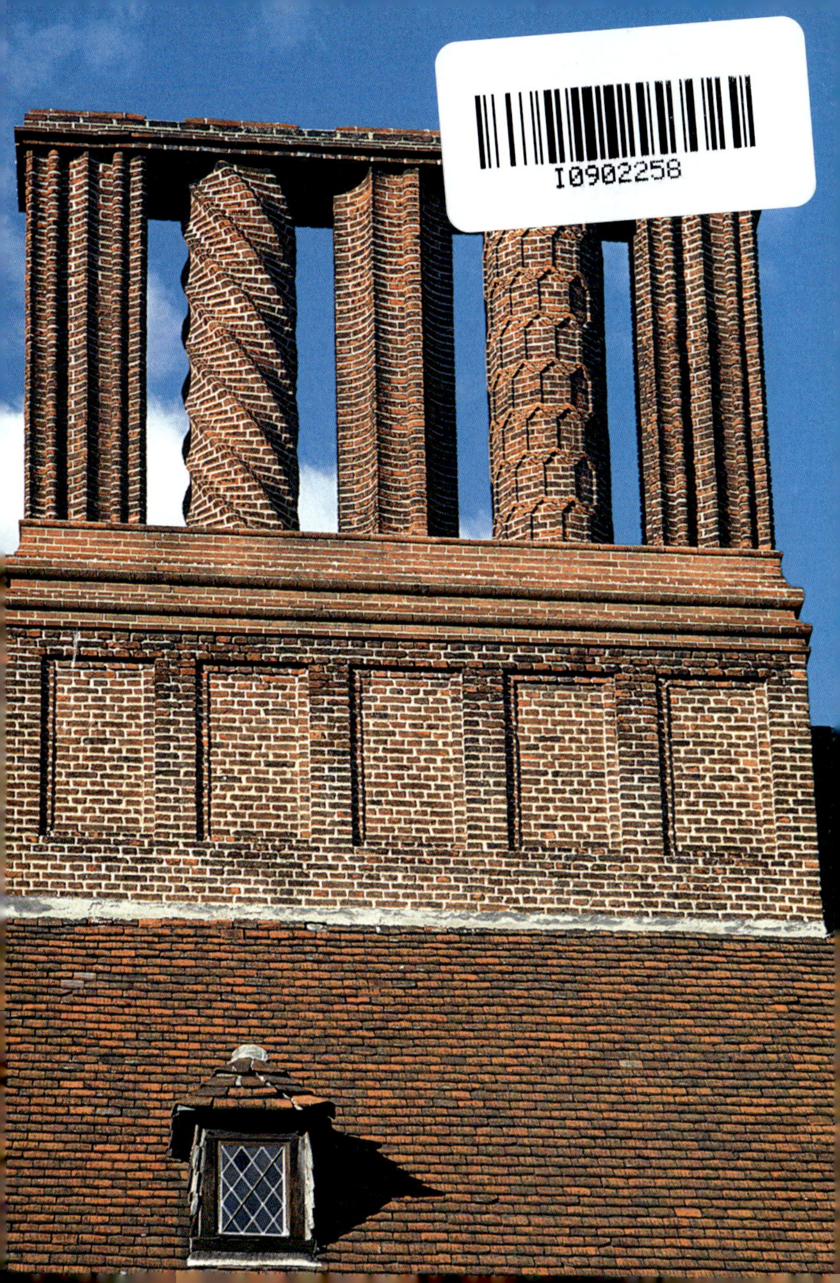

The history of Cecilienhof Palace can be traced back to 1905, when the heir to the throne, Crown Prince William, married Duchess Cecilie of Mecklenburg-Schwerin. During the summer months, the royal couple first lived at the nearby Marble Palace situated on the lake banks of Heiliger See. Designed by Carl von Gontard for King Frederick William II, the successor of Frederick the Great, this palace had been built from 1787–90. However, the building had been classified as a historical monument and lacked any possibilities to install a modern sanitary system, resulting in plans for a new residence that would be more suitable to the status of the royal couple. After the attempt to convert and enlarge Babelsberg Palace was aborted due to extremely high costs, on December 19, 1912, Emperor William II arranged for funds to be established for the construction of a new palace in the New Garden. The crown prince himself laid the foundation stone for their future residence on May 6, 1913, his 31st birthday. Shortly before the beginning of World War I, on April 13, 1914, the Saalecker Werkstätten (a group of private designers) and the Ministerium des königlichen Hauses (the ministry responsible for royal estates) drew up a contract, which provided 1,498,000 Reichsmarks as the total building sum and planned October 1, 1915 as its date of completion. Paul Schultze-Naumburg, an architect experienced in the construction of villas, was commissioned with the planning and realization of the building. He had founded the Saalecker Werkstätten in Thuringia in 1904, and had undertaken a study tour to England and Scot-

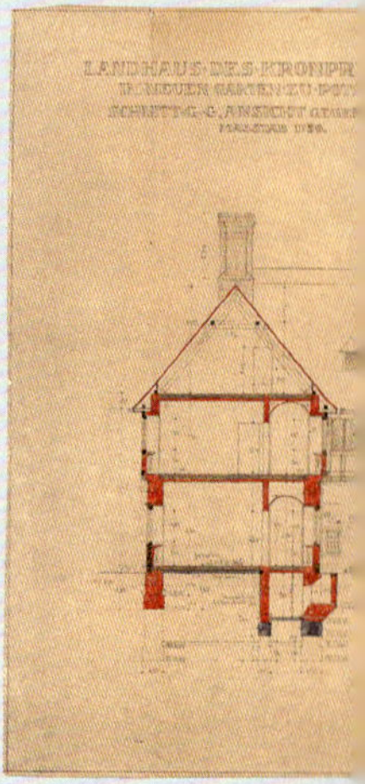

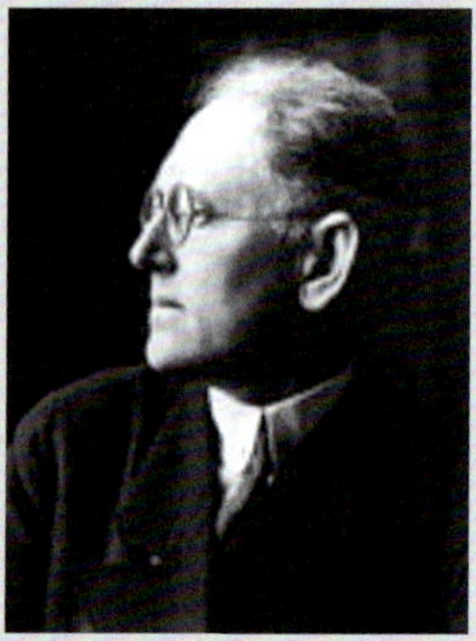

Paul Schultze-Naumburg (1869–1949)

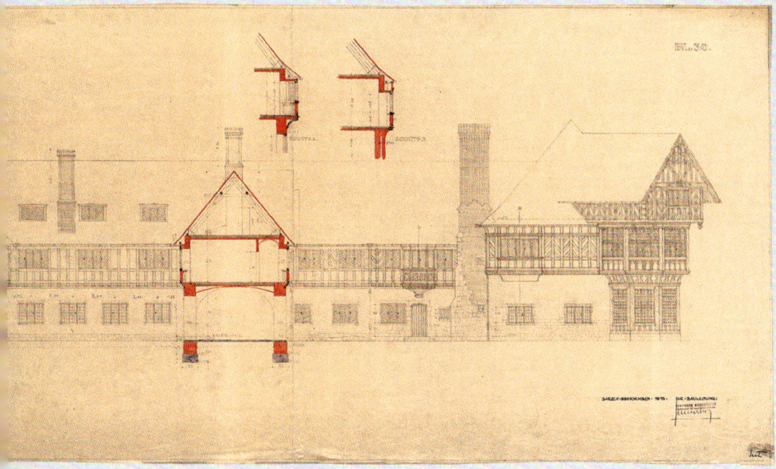

Preliminary drawing of the eastern façade, Saalecker Werkstätten, 1912

land in 1912 in the company of Count Bismarck-Bohlen, the crown prince's Hofmarschall, a court official who supervised Prussian economic affairs.

Nevertheless, the crown prince's preference for the English way of life and architecture, as well as a trip to England in 1911 presumably provided the impulse for a country manor in the Tudor style. No direct model is documented for Cecilienhof Palace; instead, typical façade elements were used, such as gables, bay windows and ornamental chimneys, as well as traditional materials such as wood, roughcast and brick.

The palace has nearly 150 rooms that are grouped around five inner courtyards. It was equipped with modern central heating, as well as numerous baths and servants' chambers. Construction had to be interrupted following the outbreak of World War I, but the completion of the interior was soon resumed in spring 1915.

The interior decoration of the grand living spaces can be attributed to well-known artists and archi-

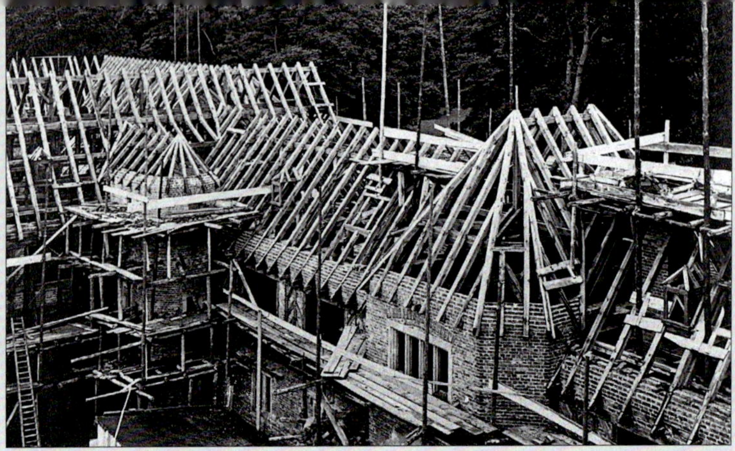

View of the roof construction during the building phase, 1914

tects, such as Joseph Wackerle and Paul Ludwig Troost. The crown princess moved into the palace on August 14, 1917, because she wanted to give birth to her sixth child there. Construction continued until 1918, and ceased with the November Revolution in Germany and the fall of the monarchy on November 9, 1918. Cecilienhof Palace is therefore the youngest and also the last structure to be built during the Hohenzollern reign. It represents an important art-historical climax in the evolution of palace architecture in Berlin and Potsdam, which had begun in the late 17th century.

The crown princess and her children waited out the political changes at Cecilienhof until November 26, 1920, then relocated their main residence to the Silesian town of Oles (now Oleśnica), near Wrocław, while her two oldest sons, Princes

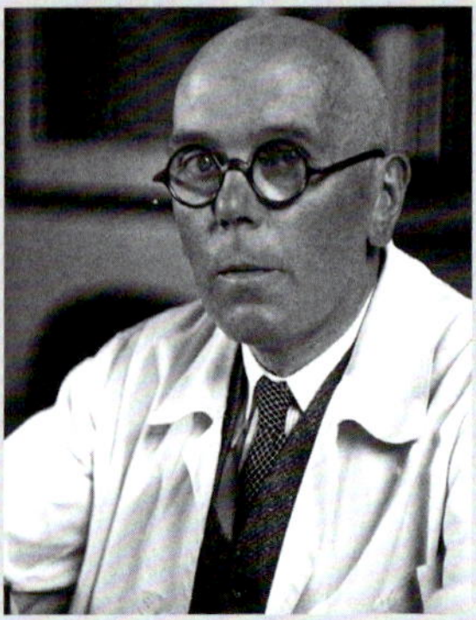

Paul Ludwig Troost (1878–1934)

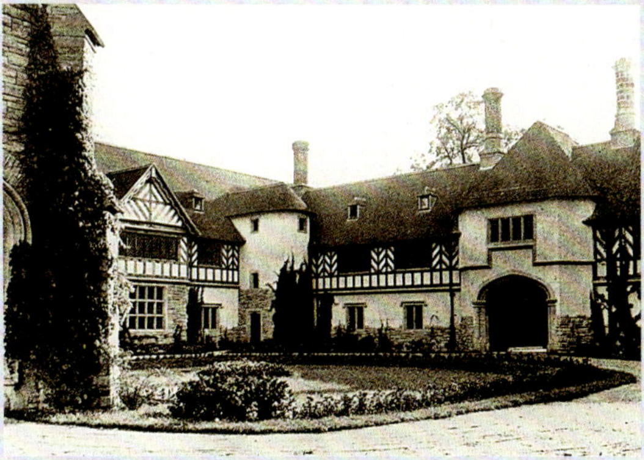

Cecilienhof Palace, Court of Honor, c. 1920

William and Louis Ferdinand, stayed behind to maintain the right of residence in Potsdam. Crown Prince William went into exile in neutral Holland on November 13, 1918, where he was interned on Wieringen, a secluded North Sea island. He remained in exile on this austere island until 1923, where his wife was only allowed to visit him a few times, but he quickly made friends with the native population. It was there that he met with Gustav Stresemann in fall 1921 and expressed his desire to be allowed to return to Germany as a private individual. Following Stresemann's appointment as German Chancellor on August 13, 1923, the crown prince received permission to reenter Germany, but only on the condition that he would refrain from any political activity. On November 9, 1923, he left his place of exile and traveled directly to Oles, where the family celebrated Christmas together for the first time in five years. Soon thereafter the royal couple decided to move back to Potsdam. Although Cecilienhof had been nationalized – like all other palaces – the crown prince received the right of residence on October 29, 1926, based on the law governing the property dispute between the Prussian state and the members of the Prussian Royal House.

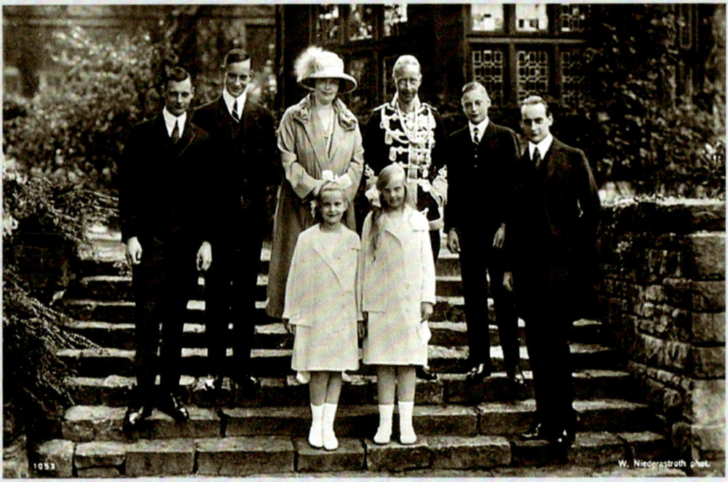

The family of the crown prince (1927)

However, the right was limited to three generations. Shortly before this date, the financial situation of the House of Hohenzollern had considerably improved during the course of a failed referendum for expropriation without compensation on June 20, 1926, which soon led to individual compensation agreements that allowed the crown prince's family to return to a life more customary to their social standing.

Cecilienhof Palace not only developed into a meeting place for the high society of Berlin and Potsdam, but also into a favorite spot for prominent artists and politicians, such as the actors Max Reinhard and Otto Gebühr, as well as the pianist Elly Ney and the conductor Wilhelm Furtwängler. A young Herbert von Karajan also accepted an invitation of the crown prince and his wife. Well-known diplomats and ambassadors from many different countries, high-ranking military officials and respected business tycoons all visited the palace.

The crown prince's hope of being able to actively participate again in political events was rekindled with the National Socialist seizure of power. He first received Adolf Hitler at Cecilienhof in 1926, and later other politicians of the Third Reich, such as Göring, Goebbels and Ribbentropp, as well as the Italian dictator Mussolini. Thus, William openly demonstrated his sympathy for National Socialist ideology. After his own attempt to run for office against Hindenburg in the 1932 German presidential elections (in Hitler's place) had failed, due to the objections of his father living in exile, he supported Hitler's rise to Chancellor of the Reich through a personal call for an election. On March 21, 1933, the Day of Potsdam, the crown prince officially took part in the inauguration celebration for the newly elected German Reichstag at Potsdam's Garrison Church. He sat behind the traditional seat of the emperor, which remained empty.

Hitler paid him another visit at Cecilienhof Palace on the same day. Their third and last meeting in 1935 ended in strife, however, when Hitler apparently declined William's wish to restore the Hohenzollerns. In consequence, the crown prince increasingly dissociated himself from the National Socialists, and was forced to recognize that his hopes for a monarchy would remain unanswered and that he would remain without influence. Nevertheless, he did not join the resistance of leading Wehrmacht generals and was not involved in the assassination attempt on Hitler on July 20, 1944. Instead, he warned his second

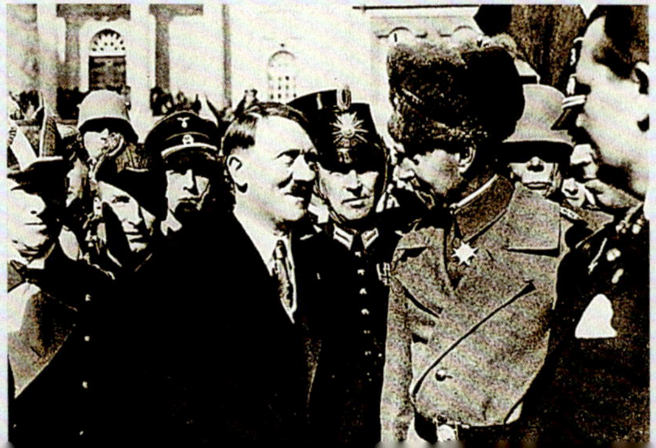

Crown Prince William with Adolf Hitler in front of the Garrison Church on the "Day of Potsdam", March 21, 1933

eldest son, Prince Louis Ferdinand, against being associated with any members of that movement. The mere suspicion of Hohenzollern participation in the conspiracy led to the crown prince coming under the watch of the Gestapo and Cecilienhof Palace being placed under surveillance.

In contrast, Crown Princess Cecilie committed herself to diverse charitable organizations and also took over the patronage of the Bund Königin Luise (Queen Luise League). After the National Socialists dissolved these associations, which also resulted in the loss of all offices connected with them, family celebrations became the only occasions for public appearances. One of these events was the wedding of Prince Louis Ferdinand and Kira of Russia, the youngest daughter of Grand Duke Cyril, the head of the House of Romanov, on May 2, 1938 at Cecilienhof Palace. Prince William, the oldest son of the crown prince and princess, died two years later on May 26, 1940, three days after he had been seriously wounded at the front in France.

On January 16, 1945, the crown prince traveled to Oberstdorf in Bavaria to take a cure for his liver and gallbladder troubles, and from there to Baad, in Austria, where he was arrested by French troops. He chose Hechingen (Baden-Wurttemberg) as a future place of residence, where he died on July 20, 1951, in a house at the foot of the ancestral Hohenzollern castle. The crown princess left Potsdam on February 1, 1945 and found temporary accommodation at the Villa Fürstenhof in Bad Kissingen (Bavaria). Having recently moved to Stuttgart in 1952, she died on a trip to Bad Kissingen on May 6, 1954, the birthday of her late husband. The couple officially separated after the end of World War II, although privately they had gone their separate ways many years before. Their last encounter took place in Hechingen on June 21, 1949, at the wedding of Princess Cecilie, their

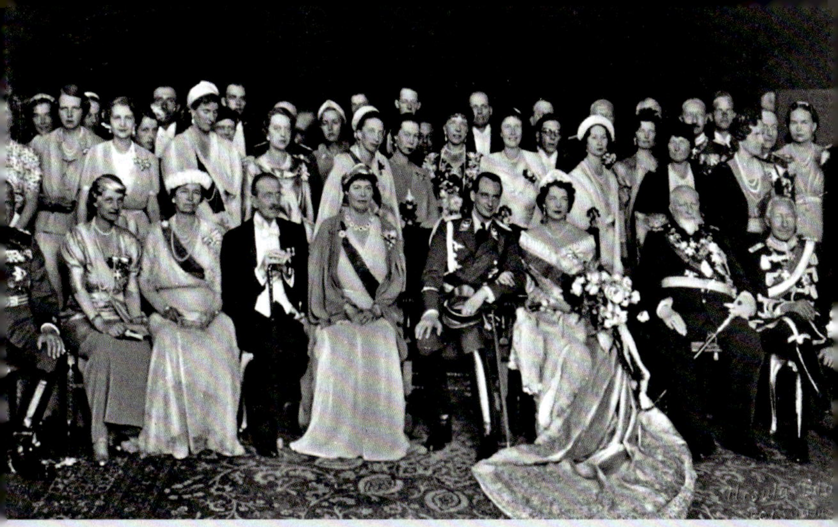

Wedding of Prince Louis Ferdinand and Kira of Russia, May 2, 1938

youngest daughter, to the American interior designer Clyde K. Harris.

Their third oldest son, Prince Hubertus, died from a ruptured appendix on April 8, 1950, in Windhoek (now Namibia). His younger brother, Prince Frederick, moved to England in 1937, where he married Lady Brigid Guinness, a daughter of the well-known Dublin brewery owner. The crown prince and princess' oldest daughter, Princess Alexandrine, suffered from Down's syndrome. She remained in the care of the family until 1936, when her place of residence changed to Lake Starnberg.

After Cecilienhof Palace had to be abandoned on April 12, 1945, due to the advance of the Red Army, and the entire collection of precious furniture as well as valuable works of art had to be left behind, it was occupied by Soviet troops on April 26, 1945. Soon afterwards, it was selected and prepared as the venue for the summit conference of the victorious powers of World War II.

Prologue

The final political act of World War II in Europe took place at the Potsdam Conference, held from July 17 to August 2, 1945, at Cecilienhof Palace. The United States of America, Soviet Union and United Kingdom met for the second time to discuss the postwar order of Germany and Europe. This relationship of convenience had begun four years previously with the provision of urgently needed relief supplies of industrial goods and armaments to the Soviet Union. Since the German assault on the Soviet Union in June 1941, a conference marathon had ensued between the three great powers. US President Roosevelt, Generalissimo Stalin and Prime Minister Churchill convened in Moscow, Washington, DC, Cairo and Casablanca to negotiate war objectives and to discuss joint military action.

The Big Three first met in 1943 in Teheran from November 28th to December 1st. Influenced by Soviet victories in Stalingrad and Kursk, Germany's capitulation in North Africa and the Allied landing in Italy, they were already focusing on postwar plans for Germany. It soon emerged that changing frontiers would

Stalin, Roosevelt and Churchill in Teheran, 1943

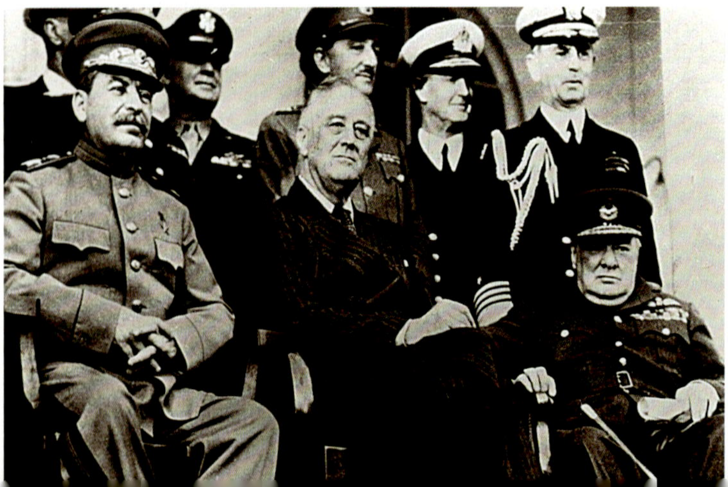

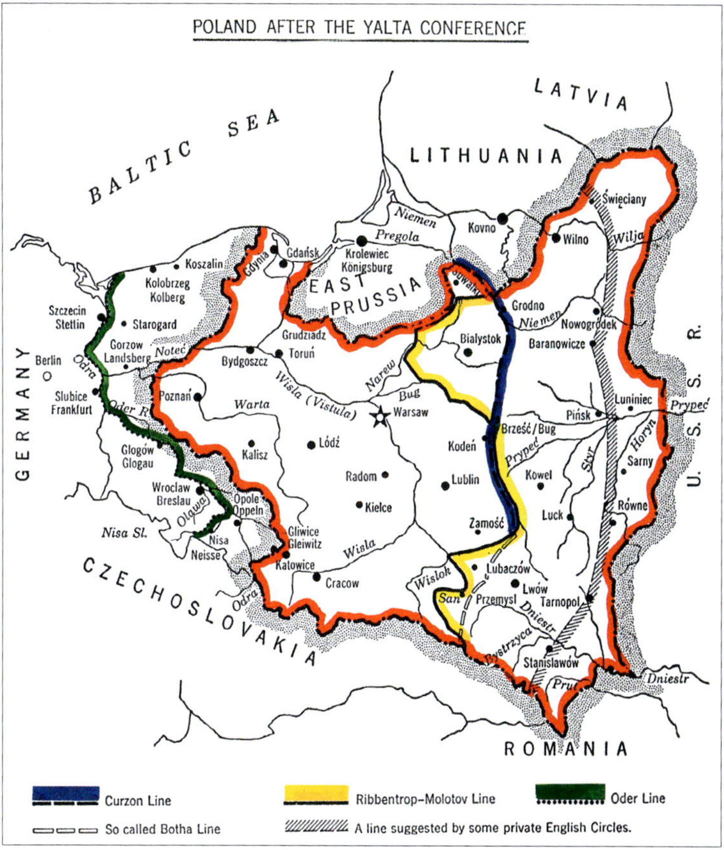

Westward shift of Poland's frontiers

affect Germany and Poland similarly. The new eastern border between Poland and the Soviet Union was to follow an ethnic boundary known as the Curzon Line. The resulting loss of over 170,000 square kilometers was to be compensated by offering land in the West up to the Oder River in return. Northeastern Prussia and Königsberg (Kaliningrad) were designated as territory to be added to the Soviet Union.

The Big Three were also in agreement that Germany was to be carved up into several small states, and Austria was to regain its sovereignty within the borders of 1937. At the end of the conference, Stalin was assured by the Western Allies that his main objective, a second front for France, would be honored.

When Operation Overlord, the long-awaited pincer movement on the German Empire was finally unleashed in June 1944, the power-political situation in Europe changed dramatically. Until the end of 1944, Stalin had controlled almost all of Eastern Europe, while the Western Allies were able to liberate France and Belgium and advance towards the Rhine. This called for a discussion on the establishment of zones of influence in Europe, which simultaneously created a strain on the Alliance. As bilateral talks on this issue between Stalin and Churchill proved inconclusive, another trilateral summit became imperative.

From February 4–11, 1945, the Big Three met in Yalta on the Crimean Peninsula, where they adopted the Declaration on Liberated Europe, guaranteeing the self-determination of all liberated peoples (based on the Atlantic Charter) and pledging to solve pressing needs. In doing so, serious differences of opinion regarding Poland came to light. The pro-Soviet and Communist Lublin Committee was competing with the Polish government in exile in London for sole representation of the country. After difficult negotiations, the three great powers finally agreed to the formation of the Provisional Polish Government of National Unity with representatives from both camps. While a compromise had been reached on paper, there were already signs that Poland would set a socio-political precedent. The Western notion of democracy came up against Stalin's socialist model of a "people's democracy".

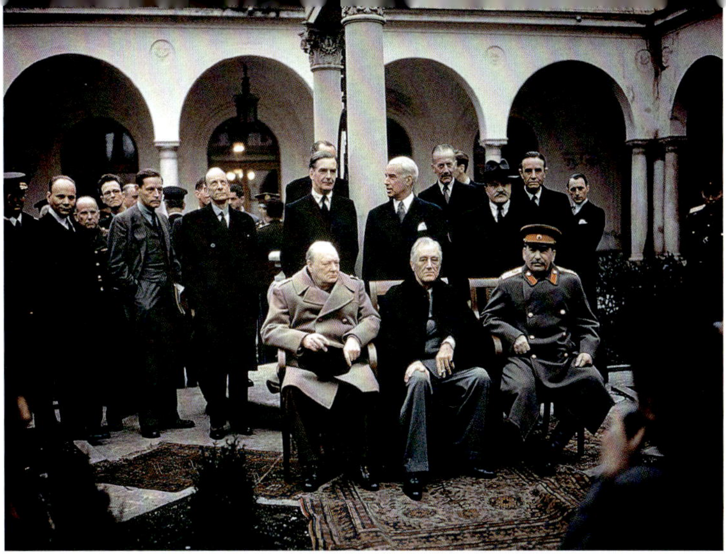

Yalta Conference, February 1945

With certain victory over Hitler in their sights, the Allies agreed to divide Germany into four occupied areas that also included France.

On the issue of compensation, which Germany was to render as war reparations, a compromise formula was found. Although a concrete sum of 20 billion dollars was named, it was only discussed as relating to any future work carried out by the Allied Commission on Reparations. On this matter also opposing viewpoints were glossed over with considerable difficulty.

However, they all agreed that the war against Japan was to be ended with the aid of Soviet troops, with Stalin agreeing that his country would enter into the Pacific War no later than three months after the end of the war in Europe.

Together they decided to establish the United Nations, the future peace organization based on the Atlantic Charter of 1941. Hence an important American objective got off the ground during the lifetime of Roosevelt, who was gravely ill. The American president did not live to see the signing of the UN Charter on June 26, 1945. He died on April 12, 1945, being succeeded by his vice president, Harry S. Truman, whose lack of foreign policy experience and more uncompromising attitude towards Stalin would complicate future negotiations.

Preparations for the Potsdam Conference

With the Berlin Declaration on June 5, 1945, the four victorious powers assumed governmental power over Germany. Based on this agreement, the most urgent problems such as the maintenance of order and administration of the country could be ensured. However, larger questions regarding postwar politics had to be decided by the heads of state at a personal meeting.

This is how the last and most lengthy conference among the Big Three, officially named The Berlin Conference (Berlin having been chosen as the conference venue) was to come about. However, the immense structural damage that Berlin had suffered from the war meant that the meeting had to be moved to neighboring Potsdam, whose palaces and historic parks had largely been spared.

As its location between two lakes Heiliger See and Jungfernsee was also ideal from a security point of view, Cecilienhof Palace in the New Garden was chosen as the central conference venue. Nearby Berlin-Gatow airport provided the necessary infrastructure. Delegations consisting of several hundred people were housed in the Potsdam district of Babelsberg, which, like Cecilienhof Palace, was divided into American, Soviet and British sectors. Each delegation used a separate entrance to access the venue.

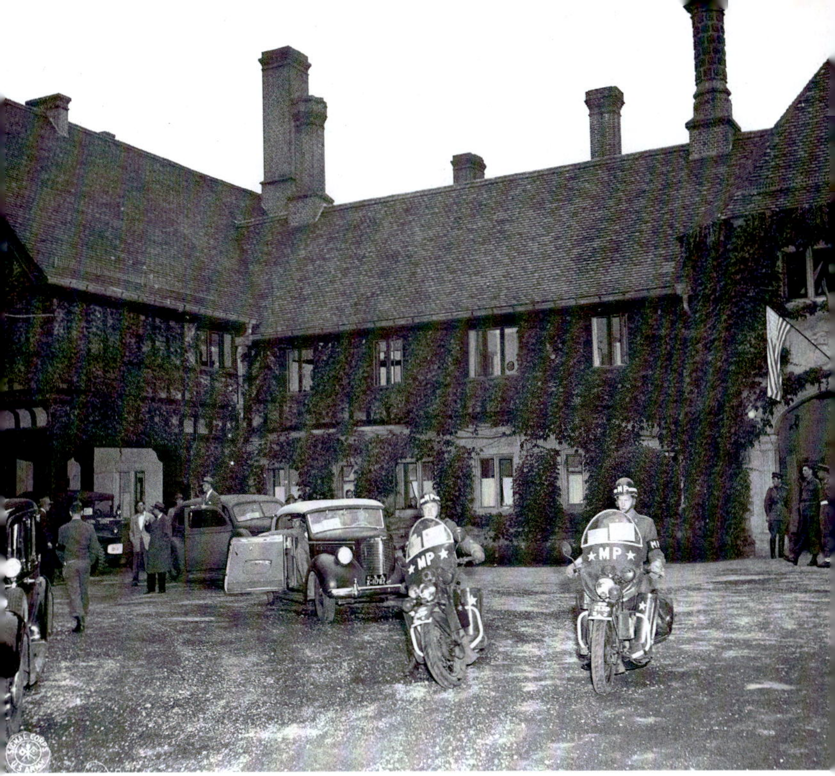

President Truman's motorcade in front of Cecilienhof Palace

As Potsdam was in the Soviet occupation zone, the conference preparations were in Soviet hands. The road network, water and electricity supply systems were all restored. Even Potsdam's parks were spruced up with plants and various horticultural arrangements, such as the red Soviet star of geraniums in the courtyard of Cecilienhof Palace. In the palace itself, there was much to be done putting 36 rooms in order, for which furniture had to be borrowed from other palaces in Potsdam and Berlin.

A newcomer (Truman) and two old acquaintances (Stalin and Churchill) initiated the bargaining marathon (also known as "Terminal") on July 17, 1945.

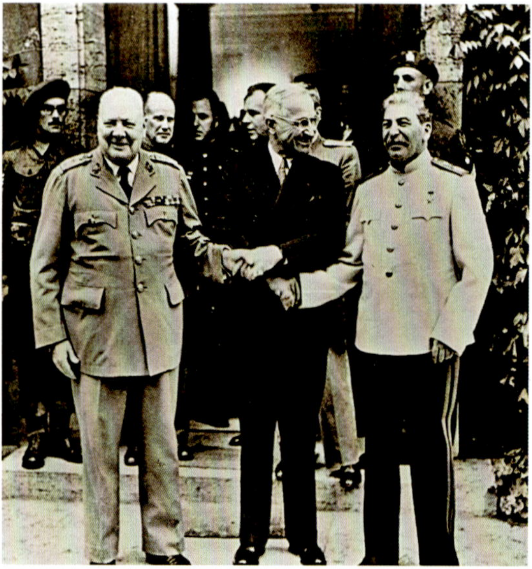

The Big Three
in Potsdam

Resolutions

The thirteen meetings characterized by heated and cumbersome negotiations were about nothing less than restructuring Europe, and how Germany was to be dealt with politically and economically. All three parties agreed on the fundamental need for denazification: The National Socialist German Workers' Party (NSDAP) was prohibited and all Nazi laws repealed. As a direct consequence, in November 1945 court proceedings were begun against major war criminals of the Third Reich at the international military tribunal in Nuremberg.

The appointment of the Allied Control Council for Germany, which met for the first time on July 30, 1945, established a body for implementing the complete disarmament and demilitarization of Germany, reconstruction of German political life on a demo-

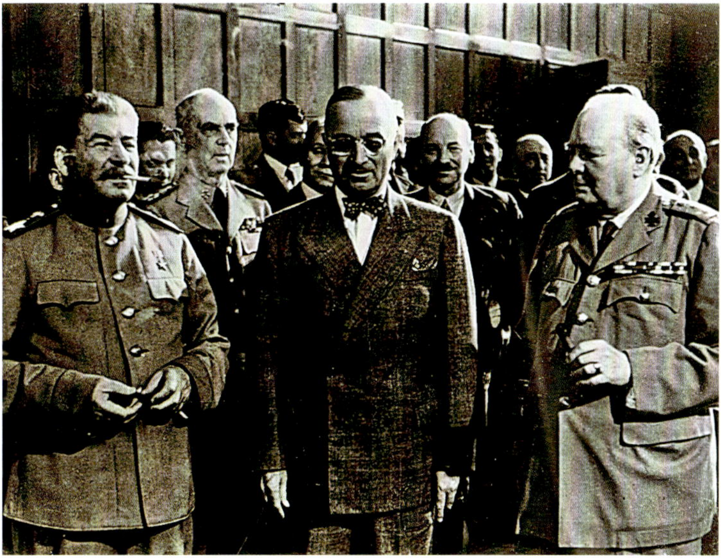

Stalin, Truman, Churchill and Attlee in the Conference Room

cratic basis and decentralization of the German economy.

The general term "democratization" was not specified in more detailed terms in order to avoid differences of opinion about its definition. However, the resolutions that were passed regarding the reparations were much more concrete: each occupying power was to satisfy its reparation claims exclusively from its own zone of occupation. In addition, the Soviet Union was to receive 25 percent of the redundant industrial equipment from the Western territories, of which 15 percent were in exchange for food and raw materials from their own occupied territories. Hence, the Allies did take into account that the zones of occupation would be taxed differently, although on paper all would be adhering to the economic unity of Germany. As Stalin had conceded to this point, in return the United States and Great Britain accepted

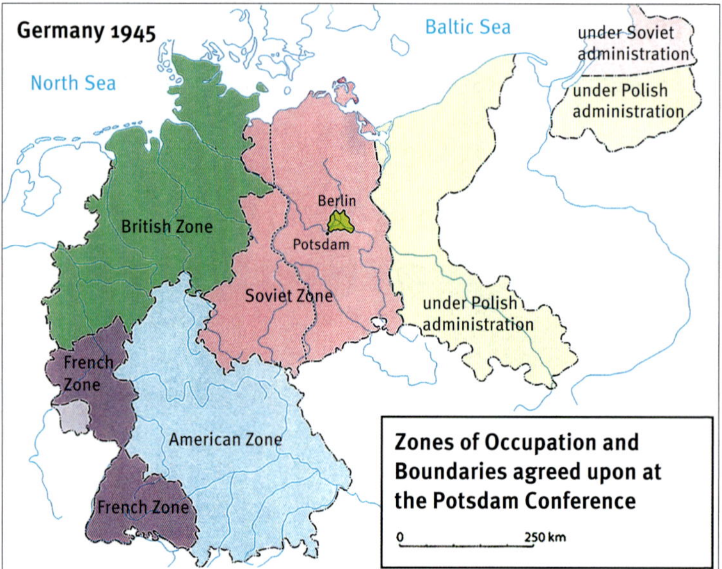

······ Provisional demarcation line in existence until May 8, 1945, between the regions occupied by the Anglo-American forces in the West and those held by Soviet troops in the East

---· Boundaries of areas occupied by the Soviet, British, American and French forces until July 3, 1945. The border of the French occupation zone was only finalized on July 28, 1945.

–·– German border after the Potsdam Conference

Greater Berlin, a part of the Soviet occupation zone, seat of the Allied Control Council (the military occupation governing body of the four Allied Occupation Zones divided into four administrative sectors: American, British, French, and Soviet)

Saarland: from 1947, a French-controlled protectorate with limited autonomy; after 1957, following a referendum, acceded to the Federal Republic of Germany

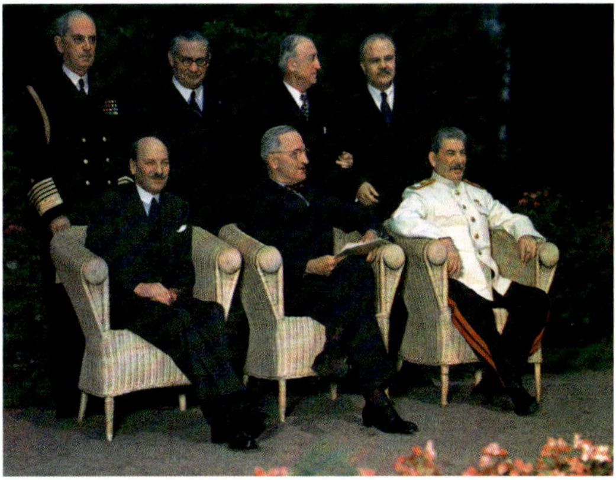

The Big Three with foreign ministers on the palace terrace, August 1, 1945

the establishment of the new German-Polish border along the Oder and Neisse rivers.

To this end, a delegation of the Polish Provisional Government of National Unity was received on July 24th at the behest of Moscow. This frontier was to be determined conclusively at a later peace conference, and until then, the German territories east of the border were not to be considered a part of the Soviet occupation zone in Germany, but as under the administration of the Polish state. Forty-five years later, on September 12, 1990, as a substitute for the peace treaty with Germany (the Two Plus Four Treaty), the Polish frontier was laid down bindingly in keeping with international law.

Occupation Zones

The Allies' decision to expel the Germans from Poland, Hungary and Czechoslovakia in an orderly and humane manner was in principle a resolution within the context of the territorial reorganization of Europe. In reality, the violent expulsion of around 12 million people resulted in a human catastrophe, shared with about 2 million Poles from the former Polish eastern territories who were forcibly resettled by the Soviet Union.

The newly created Council of Foreign Ministers included the United States of America, Great Britain, Russia, France and China. As a result of its work, peace treaties were finally signed with Italy, Romania, Hungary, Bulgaria and Finland at the Paris Peace Conference of 1946, returning the sovereignty to these states formerly allied with Nazi Germany. However, because of increasing tensions between the victorious powers, the Council of Foreign Ministers ceased to meet after 1948.

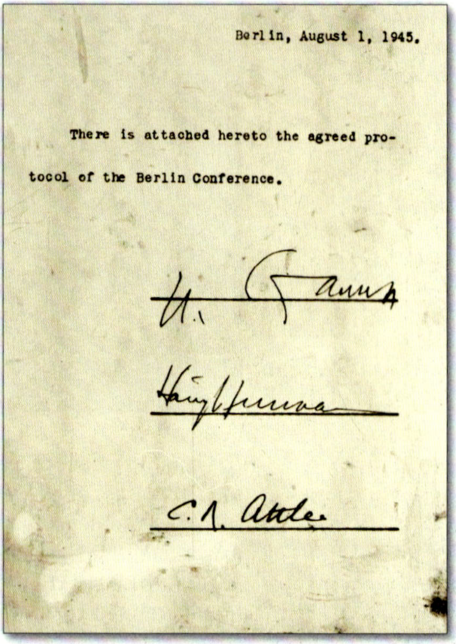
Berlin, August 1, 1945.

There is attached hereto the agreed protocol of the Berlin Conference.

Conference participants' signatures

The last summit between the Big Three ended on the night of August 2, 1945 with the signing of the Report on the Tripartite Conference of Berlin. The conference communiqué, frequently referred to as the Potsdam Agreement, does not constitute a contract according to international law.

The Potsdam Declaration and the End of the War in the Pacific

The war had ended in Europe, but military issues continued to play a major role in Potsdam. Following the success of the allied strategy, "Europe First," and the victory over Hitler, the Pacific War was now in the foreground.

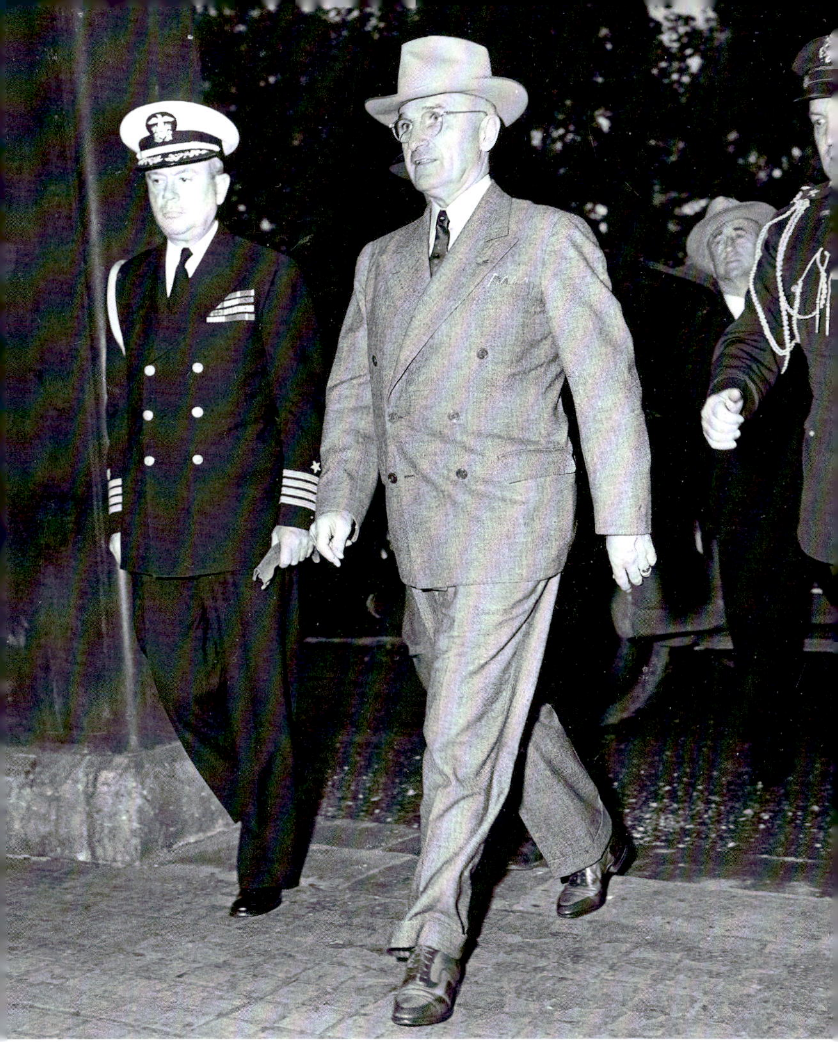

Truman entering the conference venue on July 17, 1945

Joint daily meetings were held between the British and Americans, to which the Soviet general staff were also regularly invited. After all, Stalin had agreed to enter into a war with Japan at the Yalta conference.

However, at the time of the conference Truman already held a trump card that he hoped would end the Pacific War at once – the atom bomb.

The successful testing of such a bomb in the remote desert of New Mexico on July 16, 1945, had demonstrated the efficacy of this weapon. The Potsdam Declaration, issued on July 26, 1945, was a warning to this effect. Signed by Truman, Churchill and the Chinese General Chiang Kai-shek (by telegram), it demanded the unconditional surrender of Japan. As in the case of the German Reich, it declared that war criminals would be prosecuted, the country itself occupied and demilitarized. As stipulated in the 1943 Cairo Declaration, Japanese sovereignty was to be restricted to the four main islands, or immediate and total annihilation would ensue.

The Japanese government ignored the Potsdam Declaration, whereupon in 1945 the United States dropped atom bombs on Hiroshima and Nagasaki on August 6th and 9th; actions that had, in fact, already been approved by Truman on July 24, 1945. The situation for the Japanese was hopeless: as the Soviets, as had been agreed in Yalta, declared war on them on August 8th.

On August 15, 1945, for the first time in the history of Japan, Emperor Hirohito, addressed his people directly in a radio broadcast announcing that he had accepted the demand for unconditional surrender. On September 2, 1945, the document of surrender specifically accepting the terms of the Potsdam Declaration was signed on the US battleship *Missouri* in the Bay of Tokyo.

On September 8, 1951, a peace treaty with Japan was signed in San Francisco; the fact that the Soviet Union did not cosign this declaration makes clear that these former allies had become opponents.

The Historic Significance of the Potsdam Conference

Vague resolutions, nebulous formulations and ambiguously phrased intentions characterized the Potsdam Conference; different perceptions and conflicts had already surfaced during the preliminary stages. Nevertheless, a public uproar had been successfully avoided until the end. Outwardly all the participants reassured an anxious public that the provisions of Potsdam had been a complete success.

Probably the most honest appraisal came from a conference participant who left early – Winston Churchill: "The last conference of The Big Three ended in great disappointment. Of the numerous issues raised in different meetings most went unresolved."

The conference failed because there was no longer a common Allied policy; the coalition against Hitler had won and its shared goal had been successful. However, in the moment of victory it was already carrying the seed of its own undoing: the participants' worldviews and political systems were too divergent.

If one compares the Potsdam Conference with the Big Three's conferences in Teheran and Yalta, what stands out is how much less concrete those resolutions were. Apart from the issue of reparation and uncompleted de-Nazification, few of the other declarations were implemented or were of lasting importance. Only the resettlement of large populations and the newly drawn borders were permanent, and even so it would take 45 years for the German-Polish border to be recognized according to international law.

Pages 24–25 Conference table during the first days of negotiations

One should give credit to the chief negotiators for reaching a compromise that provided future solutions. So soon after the end of the war in Europe, the Potsdam Conference could be nothing more than a

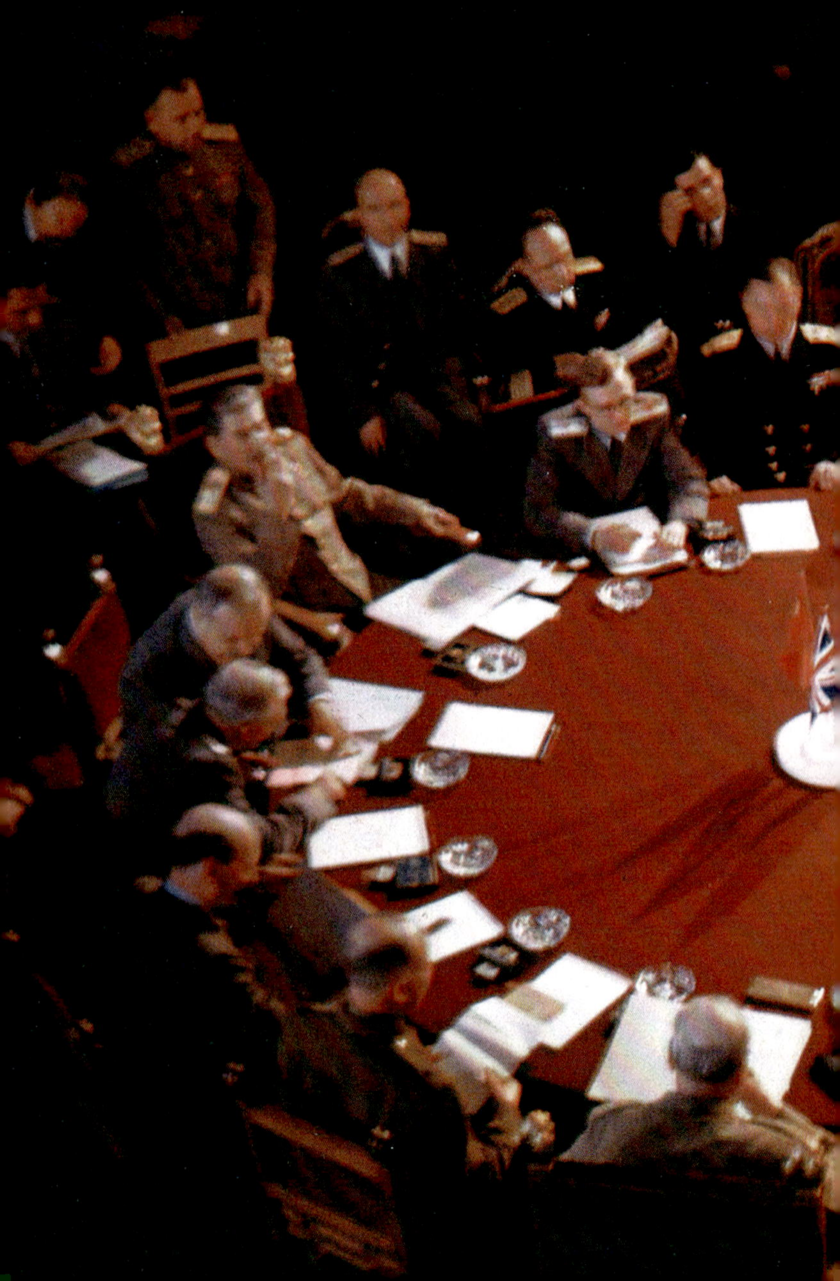

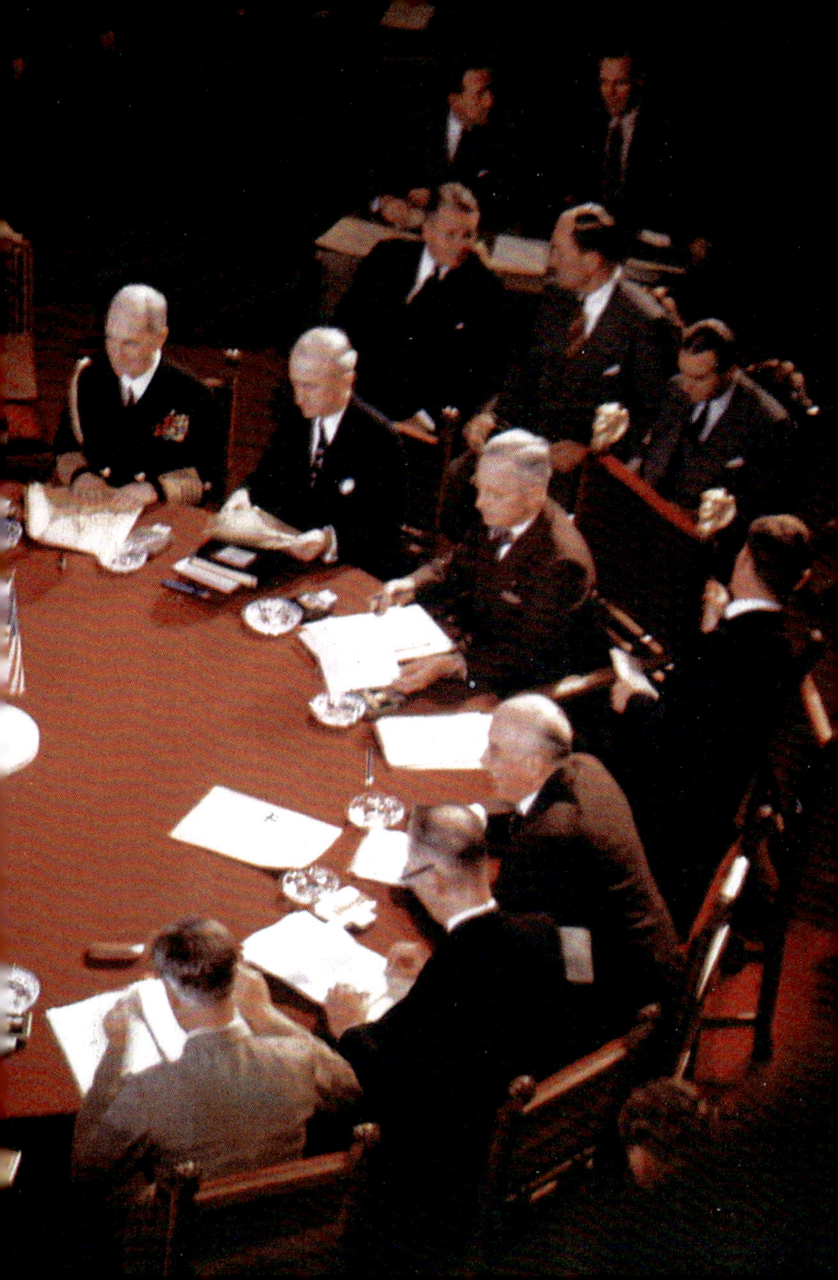

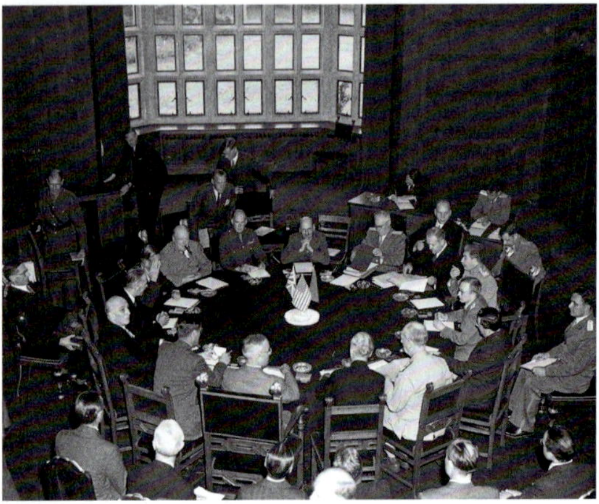

General atmosphere during the conference

beginning. The participants were well aware that this was not a peace conference. It was not for nothing that Truman ended the conference with the words: "Until our next meeting, which I hope will be in Washington." However, tensions between the victorious powers resulted in the Cold War and a division of the world into two blocs.

Negotiations to end World War I had taken more than a year; how could two weeks in Potsdam end World War II?

Ultimately, the Potsdam Conference will go down in history as the symbol of a new era initiating the Cold War and the arms race, splitting the world into a Western and Eastern hemisphere for decades to come. As Churchill had forewarned in his famous speech in Fulton, Missouri, in March 1946: "From Stettin in the Baltic to Trieste in the Adriatic, an iron curtain has descended across the Continent."

The Historic Rooms of the Potsdam Conference

The former living areas of the crown prince's family were partially refurbished and converted into workspaces and meeting rooms for the chief negotiators. This task fell to administrators of the Red Army's Rückwärtige Dienste (Behind the Lines Services), as Potsdam was in the Soviet zone of occupation, and Joseph W. Stalin thus considered the host of the conference. The required furniture was largely compiled from other palaces in Potsdam and villas in Babelsberg. Most of the original inventory was put into storage in the nearby dairy in the New Garden, where it was lost in a fire on July 18, 1945.

The tour described here deviates from the guided tour and audio guide tour. It is based on the historic sequential arrangement, which leads from the vestibule through the Great Hall and to the adjacent wings of the palace.

Vestibule (Room 1)

The sequential arrangement leads from the court of honor through the front driveway into the entrance hall, which served as a vestibule to the former living hall and conference hall. The room is divided into two areas and is dominated by a large alcove with a brick chimney. Of particular note are the panels on the walls and doors made of waxed oak, decorated with a linenfold pattern. During the conference, Winston Churchill and his successor Clement Attlee used this entrance to enter the building.

Conference Hall (Room 2)

This 26 meter-long and 12 meter-high room spans both stories of the building, and two thirds of this

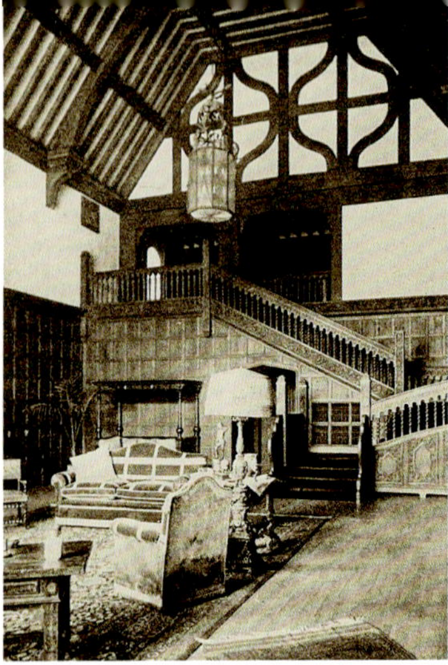

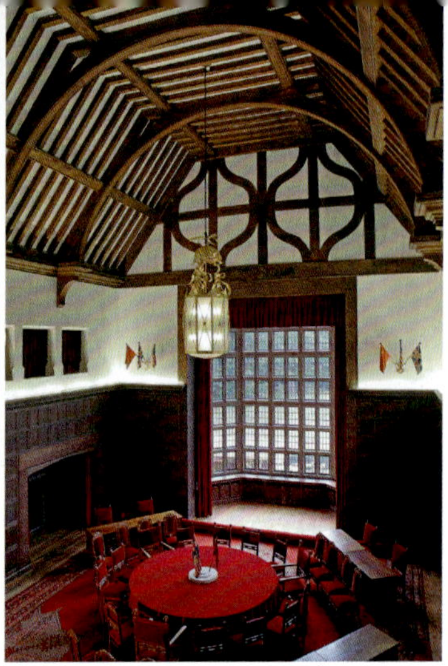

interior is paneled in oak. It was used by the royal couple and their family as a living salon and festival hall. The wood raftered ceiling, reminiscent of an inverted ship's hull, is particularly striking. The Tudor arches above the passage to the vestibule and the fireplace, as well as the sandstone alcove with 98 panes of leaded glass windows on the north side of the room, are also characteristic of the English country house style. The interior decoration initially consisted of comfortable furniture culled from other palaces or that had been in storage, which was also the case after 1918 as a result of the war. The two lanterns and the four openings on the wall above the chimney, behind which an orchestra box was set, are the only parts of the original interior decoration that still exist today.

The royal family's main living room (left)

The Conference Hall

The majestic, carved oak staircase in the Gdańsk Baroque style is a particular eye catcher. It was a present to the crown prince and princess and led to their private rooms (bedrooms, baths and dressing rooms).

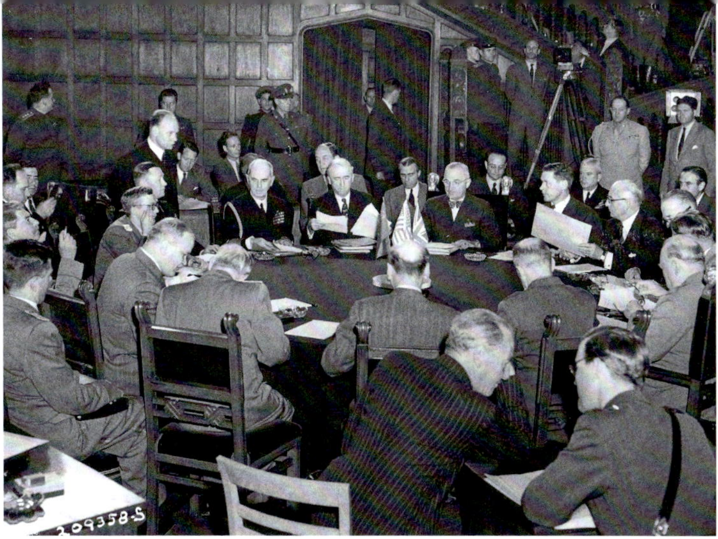

Photographers in the Conference Hall

This interior was renovated in 1945 and completely refurnished. The negotiating table with a diameter of 3.05 meters was presumably made at a Moscow furniture factory. Heads of government, secretaries of state, ambassadors and interpreters were seated on richly decorated chairs in the first row, which came from the Niederländisches Palais (Dutch Palace) in Berlin. The second row was reserved for political and military advisors, while the minute takers sat at desks.

The Big Three used the three double doors at the sides to enter the conference hall, while the middle door was only opened briefly for accredited photographers. The day started with the meetings of the subcommittees at 8:00 am, before the secretaries of state met at 11:00 am. In the evenings, deliberations of the heads of state and their delegations took place under the chairmanship of the American president Harry S. Truman.

White Salon (Room 3)

The tripartite division of this room, initially intended as a music salon, as well as its Corinthian columns and the large central rosette on the wood floor made of oak, maple and cedar, are reminiscent of the concert room at the Marble Palace. The stucco reliefs with musical emblems above the doors, created by Joseph Wackerle, emphasize its function for small

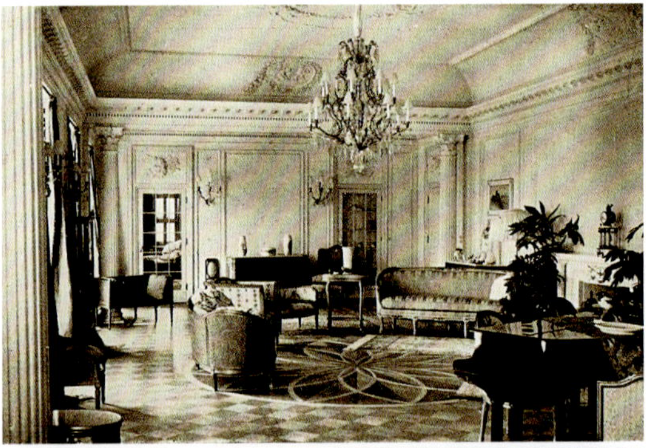

Crown Princess Cecilie's Music Salon

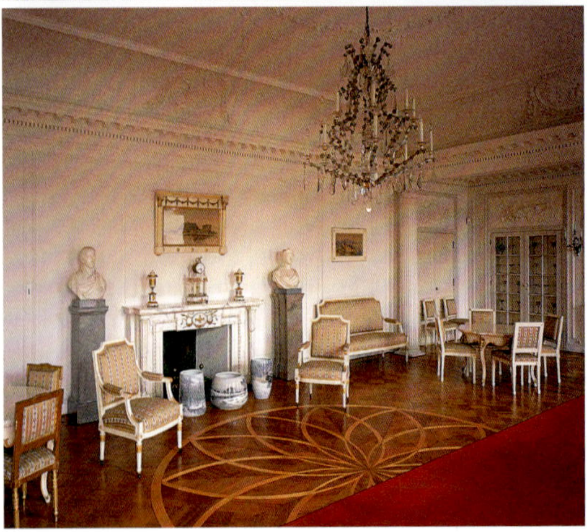

The White Salon

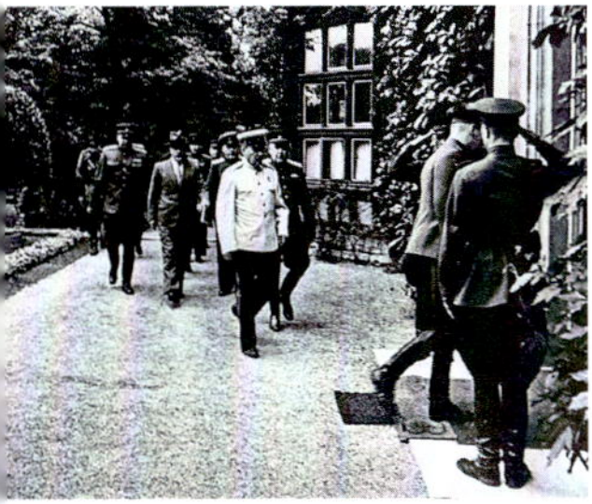

Stalin entering the White Salon

family concerts. Heating pipes are concealed behind the carved wooden veneer that encases the five windowed doors. The carvings feature figures of antique gods as grotesques that were also based on Wackerle's designs. Among the decorative elements to have survived from the original inventory are: the floor vases and flower tubs made of Petersburg porcelain, two marble busts of King Frederick William III and Queen Luise by Christian Philipp Wolff, as well as the clock and the vases on the fireplace. The chandelier and the watercolor paintings by Angelos Giallinà, depicting landscapes on Corfu and a view of the Acropolis, also belonged to the original furnishings.

Imperial porcelain and faience, as well as colored glass from the island of Murano, are exhibited in the display cases. The Rococo tables and seating furniture in the Neoclassicist style were taken from the New Palace in 1945, replacing the original interior in the style of Louis XVI. The piano has been lost since then.

During the conference, the room served as a salon for the Soviet hosts, who invited guests to a cold buffet held here on the evening of July 17, 1945. Stalin used the right windowed door to enter the palace, which was spatially divided into three separate areas, with separate entrances for each of the three delegations.

Soviet Office (Room 4)

The room referred to as the Red Salon was the writing chamber of the crown princess. The walls, originally decorated in red-patterned silk damask, had already been redecorated with a rosé-colored synthetic wallpaper in the 1930s that was restored in 2004. Nothing

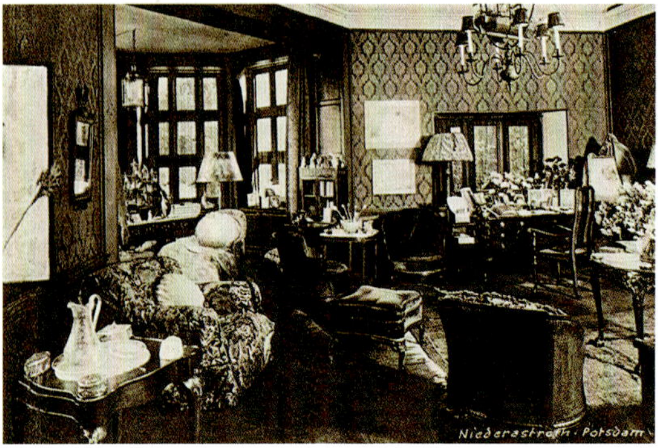

The Crown Princess' Writing Chamber

remains of the luxuriant furnishings with its many tables, armchairs and small cabinets. Only the books are part of the original décor, and they were kept – along with those in the library and the crown prince's smoking room – in the Marble Palace until the move in 1917. The bookshelves are made of mahogany, as are the wood panels and radiator covers. Blue Frisian tiles from the Netherlands adorn the fireplace, above which hangs a painting by Albert Hertel with a view of the Villa Falconieri near Rome (1911).

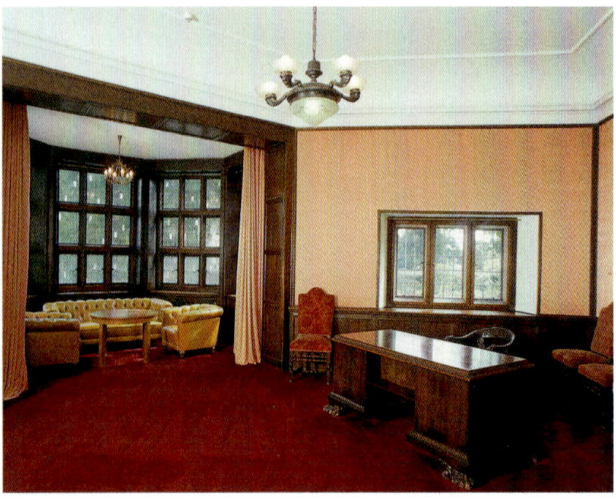

The Soviet Office

The provenance of the soft leather furniture in the alcove is just as much a mystery as that of the desk. Only the padded chairs can be traced back to the palace's Marshal Banquet Hall. However, the current arrangement of the furniture deviates from its position during the conference.

Ship's Cabin (Room 5)

A small door leads to the adjacent cabin. The interior design of this chamber that was used by the crown princess was designed by Paul Ludwig Troost, one of Germany's most prominent ship architects. It remained unchanged during the conference, and is one of the few originally preserved rooms in the palace. The maritime ambiance, which alludes to the crown princess' love of sea travel, is not only reflected in the mast and a sliding window in the

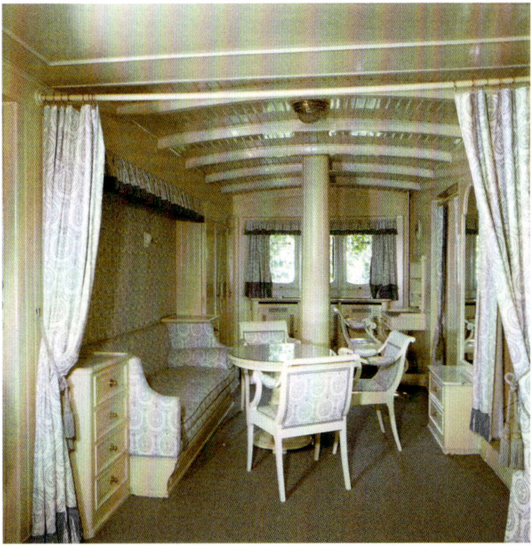

The Ship's Cabin

form of a porthole, but also in the firmly anchored cupboards and chests of drawers, as well as a washing niche concealed behind a wall display case. Like the rest of the decoration, the dainty desk was completely in line with Cecilie's taste. The wooden ceiling, walls and furniture are made of pine, painted white; the fabric wall coverings, as well as the curtains and furniture covers are made of printed blue linen. A small staircase leads to the private rooms of the crown princess on the upper floor.

British Office (Room 6)

The former living areas of the crown prince begin on the opposite side of the conference hall. Due to its function as a smoking room, the first room has a coffered ceiling made of pine, the effect of which seems somewhat gloomy in its interplay with the dark paneled walls. Nevertheless, the imposing mantlepiece and built-in oak bookcases, as well as comfortable sitting room suites and smoking tables created a cosy atmosphere.

In preparation for the conference, the furniture was replaced with pieces from the Marble Palace, which had been manufactured from mahogany at the end of the 18th century. The painting over the fireplace was painted by Hans Veit. It represents a coastal landscape on the Mönchgut Peninsula (on Rügen).

Churchill leaving the Potsdam Conference, July 25, 1945

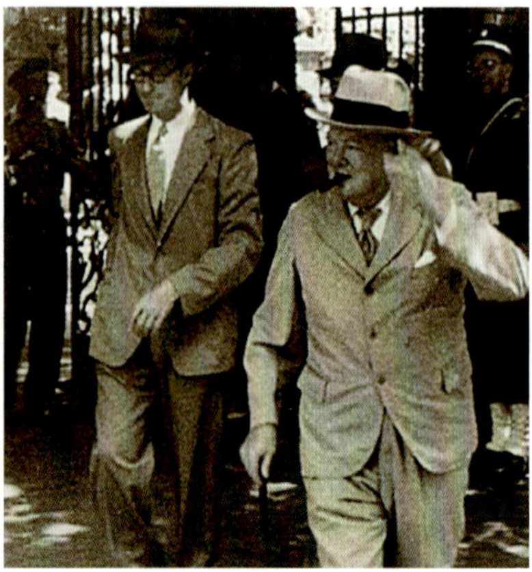

During the first phase of the conference, British prime minister Winston Churchill used this area as a consultation

Crown Prince William's Smoking Room

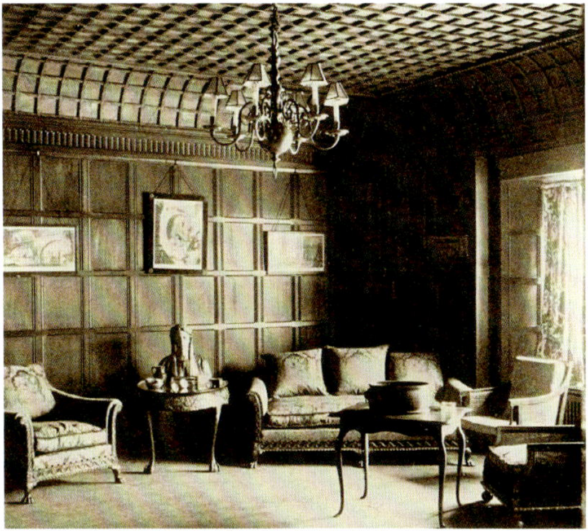

room during breaks in the negotiations. However, after the victory of the Labour Party over Churchill's Conservative Party in the House of Commons in Great Britain, Churchill did not return to Potsdam. The office was used by his successor, Clement Attlee, as of July 28, 1945.

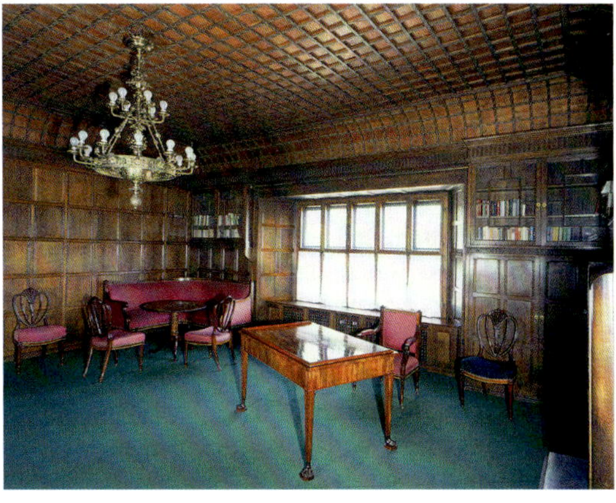

The British Office

American Office (Room 7)

The crown prince's former library was in the second room, with several built-in bookcases. While most of the books of the approximately 2000-volume inventory still exist, the collection at hand was also replaced during the preparation for the conference. The neo-Gothic desk in front of the fireplace, as well as the massive table on a central base and high armchairs in the alcove made of light maple all originate from Babelsberg Palace. They were produced during the first half of the 19th century. In contrast,

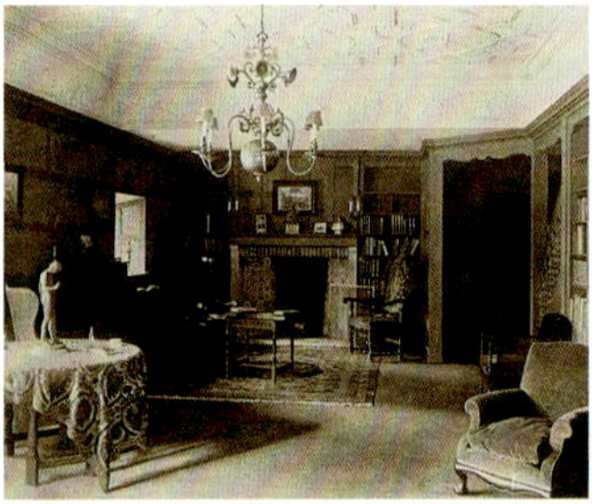

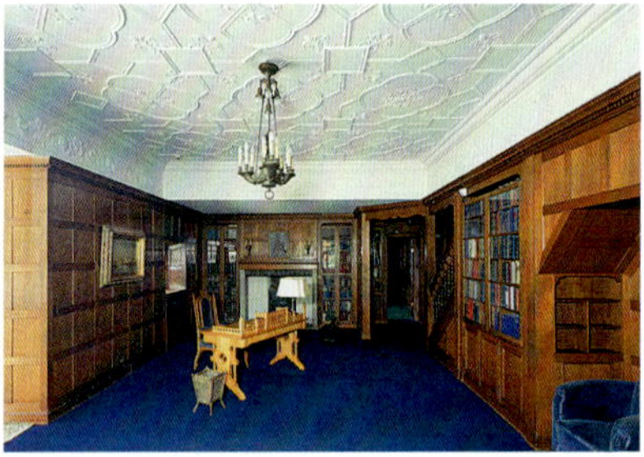

The Crown Prince's library (left)

The American Office

the provenance of the blue velvet living room suite is unknown. Unfortunately, the original decoration framing the fireplace (as seen in the photograph from the period) was replaced by plain white tiles after 1945. The painting over the fireplace by Ulrich shows an intact Kaiser-Wilhelm-Gedächtniskirche (Memorial Church) in Berlin. The view of Constantinople on the north wall, painted in 1873 by Ernst Körner, was a present from the Turkish sultan to the later Emperor Frederick III. It did not originally hang in this room.

The filigree design on the stucco ceiling and the frieze surrounding it depicting hunting scenes make a reference to the crown prince's hunting chamber located on the floor above, which could be reached by a concealed staircase.

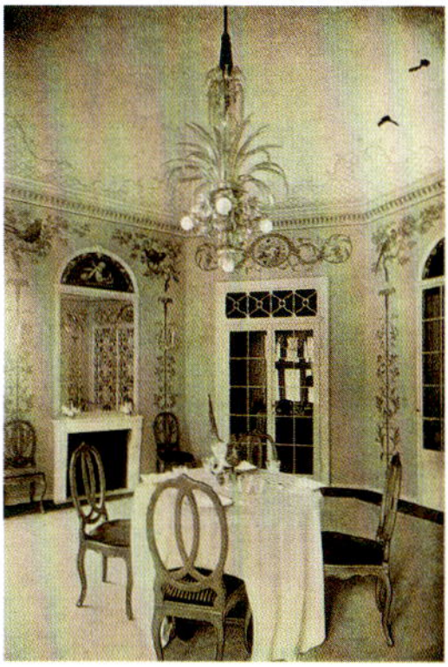

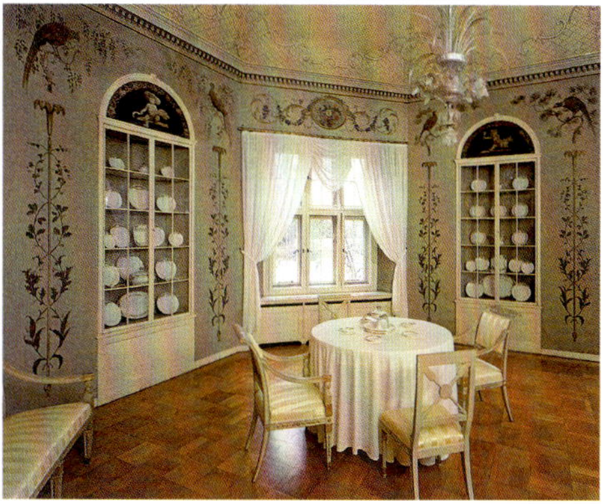

The Breakfast Room of the royal family (left)

Present condition of the Breakfast Room

This was the room American president Harry S. Truman withdrew to for meetings with his staff. Even if the 1945 missions to drop two atom bombs on Hiroshima and Nagasaki on August 6th and 9th were not decided upon here, dramatic decisions were taken during the conference to terminate the Pacific War in the Far East, which triggered a nuclear arms race between the superpowers in the East and the West.

Breakfast Room (Room 8)

The octagonal room with a vaulted dome was decorated with illusionistic flowers and bird motifs and was used by the crown prince and his family as a breakfast room. It leads to the former dining hall, which served as the palace restaurant for a number of years. The carved pine radiator cover with three doors was created by Joseph Wackerle. The Venetian crystal chandelier is an original object from when the palace was first built. Some pieces from the famous Ceres Service from 1913, made by the Königliche Porzellan-Manufaktur (the KPM Royal Porcelain Manufactory), can be seen in the display cases and on the table.

The Crown Prince and Princess' Private Suite

This area reflects the building's original use as the residence of the German crown prince, and provides excellent insight into the stately culture and modern interior design typical of the early 20th century. The suite consists of a large bedroom, two dressing rooms with adjacent bathrooms and a private room that opens onto a gallery with access to all other rooms. The broad staircase in the Gdańsk Baroque style in the main hall leads to the living area on the upper floor.

The starting point is a large portrait of Cecilie by Caspar Ritter from 1908. A second version of the painting was to be found on the passenger liner *Crown Princess Cecilie* belonging to Norddeutsche Lloyd, which was launched in 1906 in Stettin (Szczecin).

Upper Gallery (Room 9)

Only some of the glassware and porcelain seen here is from the original inventory of the palace, which was mainly produced by the Royal Copenhagen and Bing & Gröndahl porcelain manufactories, the market leaders in the 19th century. To make up for losses in the collection, important art nouveau glass by Emile Gallé and the Daum Brothers, who were influenced by the Nancy School of glassmakers, is exhibited with pieces made by *Loetz* in Austria.

This collection focuses on 10 figures from the famous *Hochzeitszug* (Wedding Procession) by Adolph Amberg, a centerpiece conceived for the wedding of the crown prince and princess in 1905. This design was initially rejected by Empress Augusta Victoria, who disapproved of the permissive nudity of some of the figures. In 1908, the drawing was acquired by KPM (Königliche Porzellan-Manufaktur) and produced in several series over the years. It portrays a procession of representatives from different cultures, past and present, paying homage to the couple. The bride is represented as Europa on the bull and the bridegroom as a Roman warrior on horseback. The centerpiece originally consisted of 20 figurines, and is considered a preeminent masterpiece of art nouveau.

At the end of the gallery is a 1936 portrait of Crown Prince William painted by Fritz Reusing.

The Crown Prince's Dressing Room (Room 10)

Compared to the more prestigious living area on the ground floor, the private quarters are informed by comfort and functionality. Despite their seeming simplicity, they impress as being much more sumptuous and elegant, due to the preciousness and high-quality craftsmanship of the materials used. The furniture and walls of the crown prince's dressing room are made of Thuya burl, palisander and pear wood veneer.

The full-length wood paneling concealing doors, cupboards and a safe, demonstrates the ingenuity of the interior design, which aims for a coherent overall effect and does not reveal the different functions at first glance. However, only a small table and desk chair from the original furnishings survive. The missing pieces have been replaced by similar items from that era, such as the desk and two armchairs.

The curtains and furnishings decorated with naturalistic motifs give an impression of the original décor. The carpet, which has been modeled after the original, has been fitted in the customary way across the entire floor. With few exceptions, all rooms, cor-

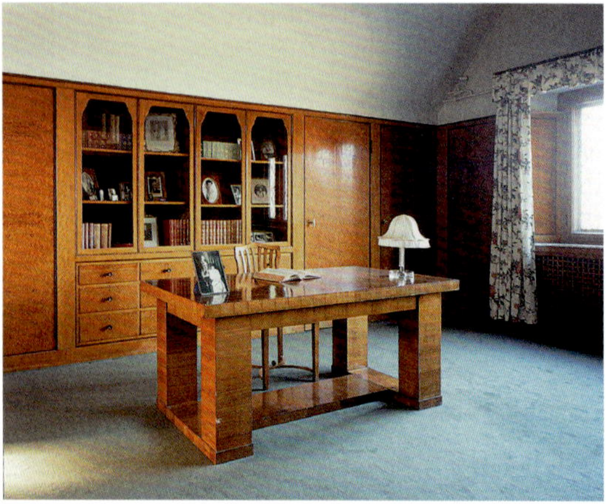

The Crown Prince's Dressing Room

ridors and stairs were carpeted. The display cases contain family photographs and on an easel stands a portrait of Crown Prince William, painted in 1932 by Bernhard Zickendraht, previously displayed in the living area on the ground floor.

Bernhard Zickendraht, *Crown Prince William*, 1931 (left)

Bernhard Zickendraht, *Crown Princess Cecilie*, 1934

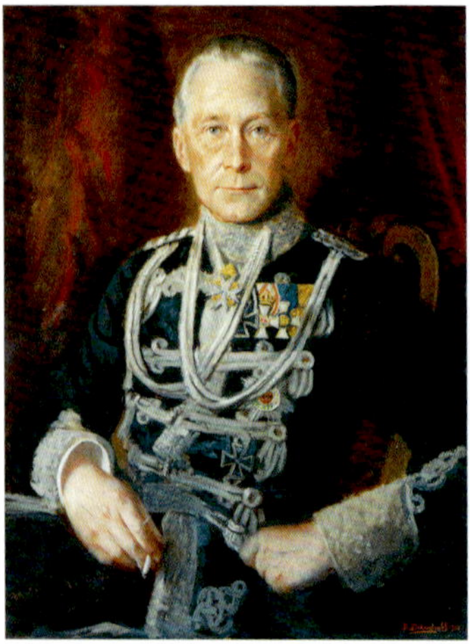

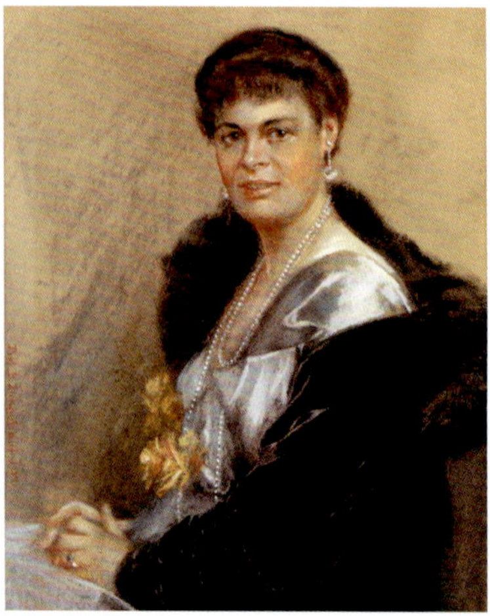

The Crown Prince's Bathroom (Room 11)

The connecting bathroom has been fitted with ceramic tiles, a sunken bathtub and a washbasin made of Schupbach limestone. The majolica relief of a nymph inserted into the tiles above the bathtub and sanitary fittings have been preserved in their original form, giving an authentic impression of the private atmosphere of the crown prince's apartment.

The Crown Prince's Bathroom

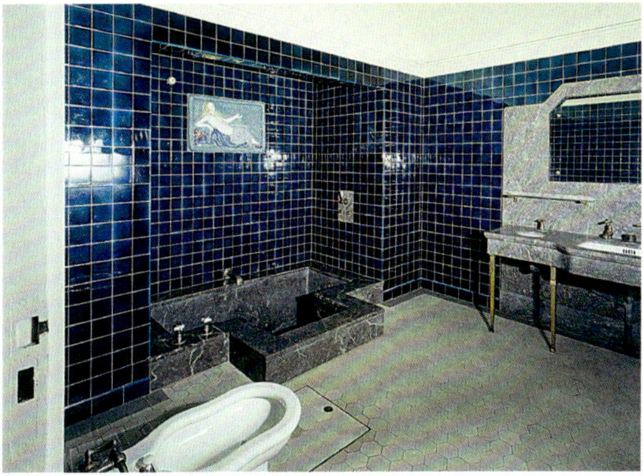

The Bedroom of the Crown Prince and Crown Princess (Room 12)

A small corridor leads to the adjacent bedroom, which in all likelihood was no longer used in common by the crown prince and princess after 1923. An alcove separated by a glass sliding door, intended as a small smoking room, had been provided for the gentleman of the house. The interior decoration is reminiscent of the interior of a ship and can be ascribed to Paul Ludwig Troost, who furnished a number of notable passenger liners for Norddeutsche Lloyd. The crown princess commissioned the architect to draw up some designs for her private chambers, after she had seen

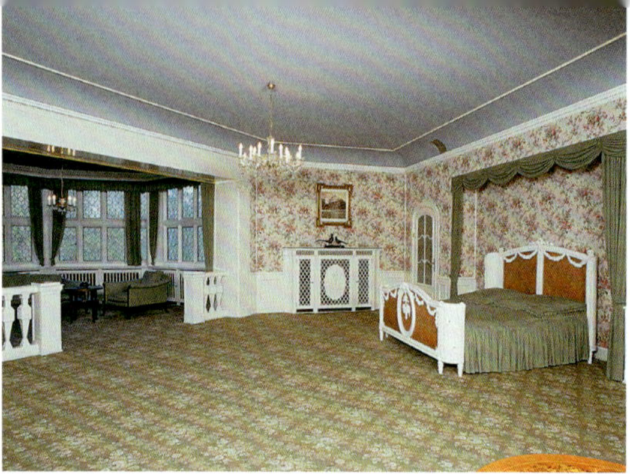

The Royal Bedroom

the interior decoration of the *Columbus*, a luxury liner she christened in Danzig (now Gdańsk) in 1914.

As the room was used as a music salon during the conference in 1945, subsequently completely refurnished and then transformed into a hotel room, only a few pieces of the original furniture could be located. They include a dresser, a corner display case and a round coffee table, whose fine wood and elaborate marquetry radiate exclusiveness. Unfortunately, only Troost's drawing of the bed survived, so that it has been replaced with a similar item of the same period from the estate of a Potsdam family. The sofa and chairs are in part from the palace inventory and were formerly used in the lower living quarters. The carved decorative wooden elements in white adorning the space above the doors and radiator covers are by Joseph Wackerle.

A 1934 portrait of Crown Princess Cecilie by Bernhard Zickendraht graces the fireplace.

A sketch by William Pape above the dresser captures the 1906 festive christening of the first-born son of the crown prince and princess, Prince William of Prussia, in the Marble Gallery of the New Palace. The lavish textile furnishing of the room is particularly impressive, and its faithful restoration evokes the interplay between the floor, walls and ceiling.

The floral motive of the carpeting, fabric wallpaper and sky-blue ceiling create the impression of a pergola.

The Crown Princess' Private Chamber (Room 13)

The pergola-like character also carries over to the upper deck of the gently curved narrow staircase that leads to the ship's cabin below and connects the state rooms on the ground floor. Another set of stairs leads to the crown princess' dressing room, where lattice bars have been superimposed at regular intervals on the rose-covered wallpaper, creating the illusion of a pavilion. Of the decorative elements finished in matt-lacquered white (also ascribed to Troost) only the built-in wardrobe and ostentatious radiator covers remain.

The Crown Princess' Dressing Room (Room 14)

This chamber is the crowning glory of this tour, as it has been almost entirely restored to its former splendor.

The veneer used for the walls and furniture is made of Russian birch. The room's uniform appearance has been heightened by using the same printed linen fabric for isolated wall panels and to upholster the furniture. The rose-hued fabric with its motifs from antiquity harmonizes with the gray flower medallions of the carpet. The decision to have some of the furniture made in St. Petersburg is due to the relationship of the crown princess to the Romanovs: her mother was the granddaughter of Nikolaus I. Two large photographs portray respectively the young betrothed couple William and Cecilie in 1904, and their four sons at the christening of Prince Frederick in 1912.

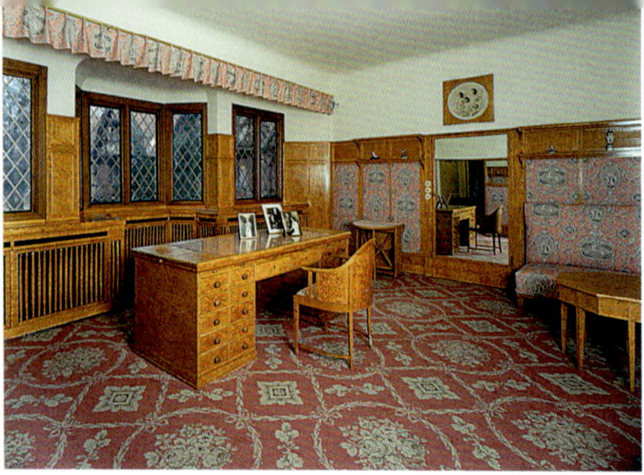

The Crown Princess' Dressing Room

The Crown Princess' Bathroom (Room 15)

The crown princess' favorite colors are also prominent in this spacious bathroom. However, apart from the antique pink tiles, only the washstand made of white Carrara marble (of which the original bathtub was also made), remains. Unfortunately, all other fixtures were lost during the temporary use of this room as a hotel bathroom.

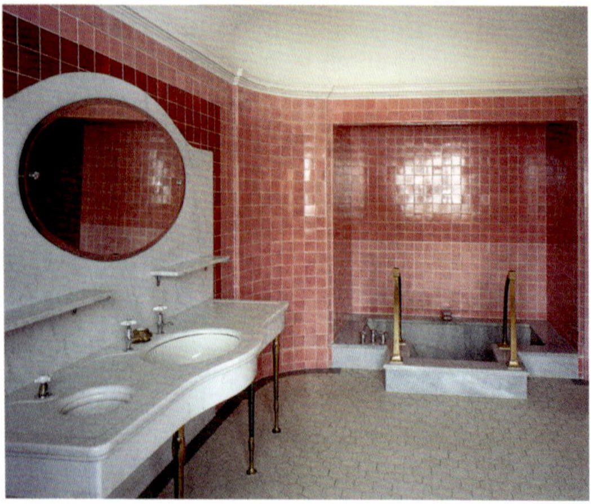

The Crown Princess' Bathroom

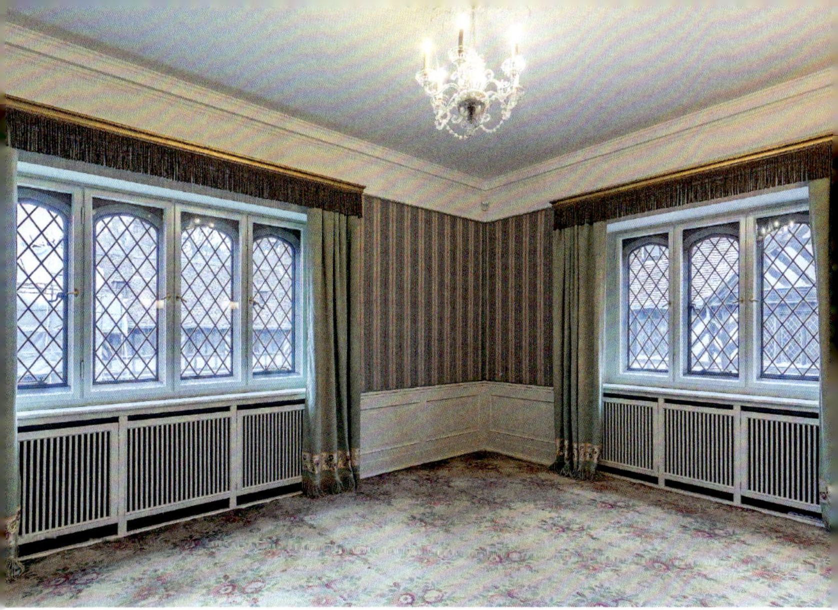

Living room of the guest apartment

The Guest Apartment (Room 16–19)

The ensemble of rooms on the piano nobile above the main entrance consists of four rooms, comprising a living room, bedroom, bathroom as well as a servant's chamber. All the interior design is the work of the architect *Paul Ludwig Troost*. The apartment was at the private disposal of noble guests of the royal couple. Among the regular guests, for example, was Cecilie's older sister, Queen Alexandrine of Denmark, during her stays in Potsdam. This royal visitor resided in Schloss Cecilienhof in 1927, when she came for the confirmation of the princes Hubertus and Friedrich, in 1936 for the Olympic games in Berlin, and again in 1938 for the wedding of the royal couple's second oldest son, Prince Louis Ferdinand, to Grand Duchess Kira of Russia. In 1932 and 1937, the queen made a stop in Potsdam in order to continue with her sister,

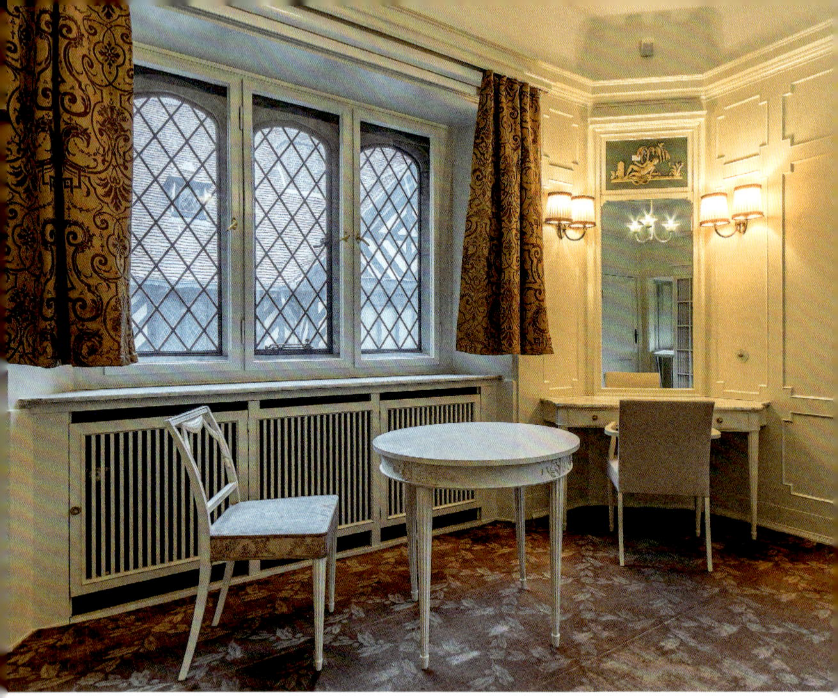

Bedroom of the guest apartment

the crown princess, to Bayreuth where they would attend the Bayreuth Festival. Presumably, in times when there were no guests, the apartment was also used by the royal couple's youngest daughter, Princess Cecilie; a 1934 photograph, made available to the Schlösserstiftung by the House of Hohenzollern, shows her standing by the fireplace. The photo also was invaluable for reconstructing the original interior design. Only a few of the original furnishings have survived: the wall closet, a vanity, two chairs, and a small table. The elegant marble fireplace in the living room and the partially reconstructed wall lamps also originate from the time that the palace was built. Of outstanding importance are the original fabrics decorating the rooms, which were put in storage in

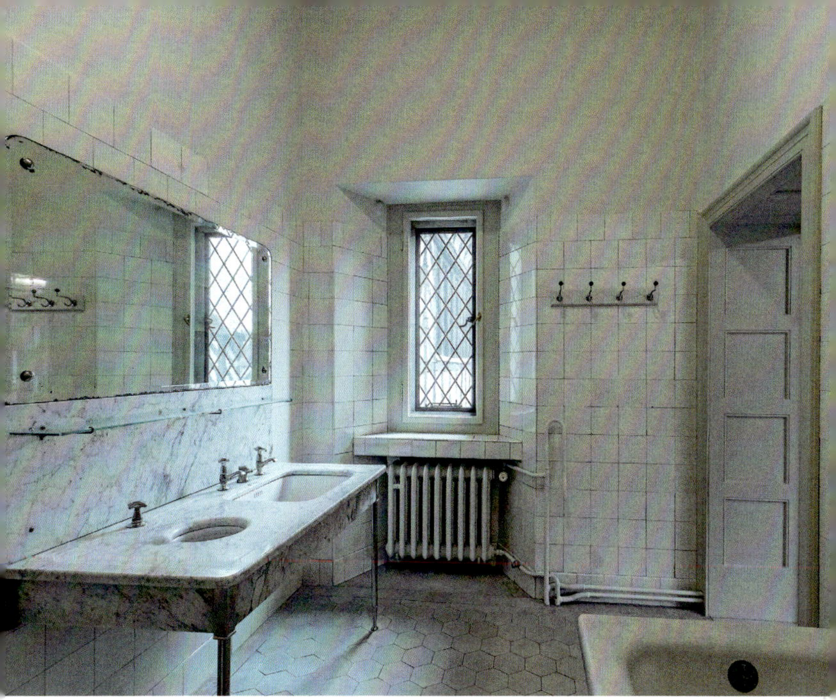

Bathroom of the guest apartment

1974. With great care, these original wall coverings and window decorations have been cleaned, the very fragile fabrics have been provided with a supportive under-layer of the appropriate colours, stitched, and installed in the rooms in accordance with their original function. The fitted carpets were laid using traditional techniques, lending authenticity to the rooms and offering an impression of elite early-twentieth-century lifestyle. In order to allow tours access to the bedroom, a particularly damaged section of the carpet was removed, so that this area could be entered by visitors, while the other rooms can only be viewed from the outside. The bathroom was carefully cleaned, missing sanitary wares and armatures were either acquired from antique stores or reproduced on the basis of old illustrations and photos. In an aide-de-camp chamber, a servant's livery from imperial times is on display in a vitrine. It was meticulously restored and, together with a photo of the wedding on May 2, 1938, offers a rare a view into royal etiquette at court. The artistic linoleum with its strip parquet design is the last remaining floor covering of this type in the palace, and is important as an exemplar of the aesthetics of the contemporary architecture of that time. On a wall plaque and stand-up displays, are photos from the 1930s, as well as drawings and designs from the estate of *Paul Ludwig Troost*.

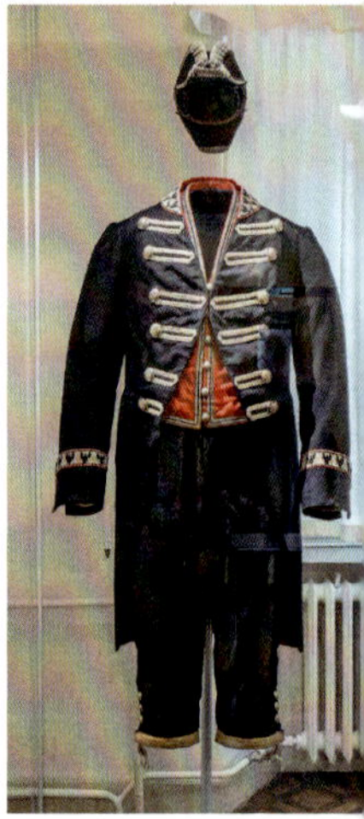

Livery in the servant's chamber of the guest apartment

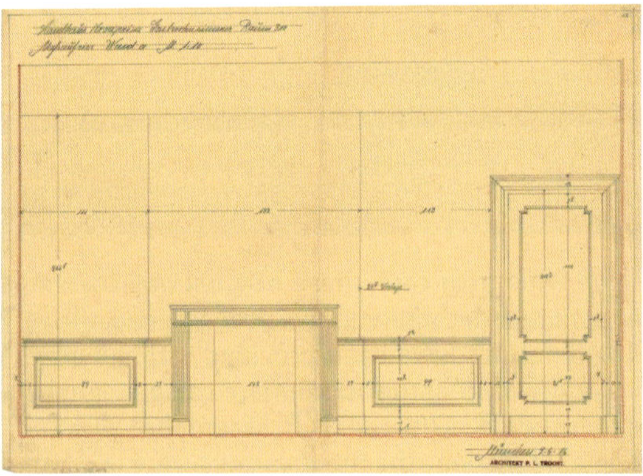

Guest Living Room. Fireplace wall. Drawn to scale, Paul Ludwig Troost, June 2, 1916.

Cecilienhof Palace
Im Neuen Garten 11
D-14469 Potsdam
Tel.: +49(0)331.96 94-520
Fax: +49(0)331.96 94-530
e-mail: neuer-garten@spsg.de

Contact
Mailing address: Postfach 601462, D-14414 Potsdam

Information:
Visitor Center at the Historic Windmill
An der Orangerie 1, 14469 Potsdam
Tel.: +49(0)331.96 94-200
Fax: +49(0)331.96 94-107
e-Mail: info@spsg.de

Opening Hours:
April–October: 8:30–6
November–March: 8:30–5

and

Visitor Center at the New Palace
Am Neuen Palais 3, D-14469 Potsdam
e-mail: info@spsg.de

Opening Hours:
April–October: 9–6
November–March: 10–5
Closed Tuesdays

Group Reservations
Tel.: +49 (0) 331.96 94-200
e-mail: gruppenservice@spsg.de

Opening Hours and Admission Prices
Cecilienhof Palace is open from Tuesday to Sunday.
Current opening hours and admission prices are listed online: www.spsg.de.
The visitor centers of the Stiftung Preußische Schlösser und Gärten Berlin-Brandenburg (SPSG) are glad to provide information regarding prices for groups, guided tours or individual arrangements. An audio guide tour of the historic sites of the Potsdam Conference is included in admission and is available in 12 languages.

The Pfingstberg is within walking distance of Cecilienhof Palace. One of the most beautiful views of Potsdam can be seen from atop this hill from the towers of the Belvedere, a structure based on designs by King Frederick William IV. It was built from 1847–63 by Ludwig Persius, Ludwig Ferdinand Hesse and Friedrich August Stüler. The nearby Temple of Pomona was built in 1800 by Karl Friedrich Schinkel. Next to the New Garden is the former Militärstädtchen No. 7, which was the KGB's command center in Germany until 1994. This detention center of the Soviet counter-intelligence at Leistikowstraße 1 was restored in 2007–08 and is now a historical site.

Public Transportation
from Berlin: S 1 or RE 1 to Potsdam Hauptbahnhof (central station)
from Potsdam Hauptbahnhof: Bus 603 to "Schloss Cecilienhof" (weekends and holidays) or any of the trams and bus lines to "Platz der Einheit/West," then change to Bus 603 to "Schloss Cecilienhof" (weekdays)

Information for Visitors with Disabilities
The historic site of the Potsdam Conference is barrier-free and wheelchair accessible. However, the private rooms of the crown prince and princess on the upper level are not barrier-free and not accessible by wheelchair.
Wheelchairs are available at Cecilienhof Palace for visitors with impaired mobility. A WC with disabled access is located nearby.
Further Information: handicap@spsg.de

Museum Shops
The museum shops at the Prussian Palaces and Gardens invite you to further explore the world of the kings and queens of Prussia – and to take that experience with you. Your purchases are in fact donations, because the profits of the Museumsshop GmbH help to support the acquisition of works of art and to augment necessary restorations of the SPSG's palaces and gardens.
www.museumsshop-im-schloss.de

Gastronomy
Café „Cecilie" im Hofgarten des Schlosses Cecilienhof
(in the summer months)
Tel.: +49(0)30.246 584 30
www.wohlthat-entertainment.de

Meierei Brauhaus im Neuen Garten (ganzjährig)
Im Neuen Garten 10
Tel.: +49(0)331.70 432 11
www.meierei-potsdam.de

Tourist Information
Tourist-Information der Stadt Potsdam
Humboldtstraße 1–2 (Am Alten Mark)
14467 Potsdam

or

Babelsberger Straße 16 (Im Hauptbahnhof)
14473 Potsdam
Tel: +49 (0)331.275 588 99
e-Mail: info@potsdamtourismus.de
www.potsdamtourismus.de

Tourismus-Marketing Brandenburg GmbH (TMB)
Am Neuen Markt 1
D-14467 Potsdam
Tel.: +49(0)331.200 47 47
e-mail: tmb@reiseland-brandenburg.de
www.reiseland-brandenburg.de

Preservation of the Historic Gardens and Their Design
The Prussian cultural landscapes in Potsdam and Berlin have been listed as UNESCO World Heritage Sites since 1990. We need your support to protect this cultural heritage and the exceptional works of art within this fragile natural environment! By behaving considerately, you will help to ensure that you and other visitors may continue to enjoy these historic gardens in all their splendor. The park regulations of the Stiftung Preußische Schlösser und Gärten Berlin-Brandenburg (SPSG) are designed to protect and conserve this unique heritage, and to assist you with how to conduct yourself appropriately and considerately. Your observation of these regulations is greatly appreciated!
We hope you will enjoy your visit to the royal Prussian gardens.

Select Bibliography

Robin Edmonds: *Die Großen Drei*. Berlin, 1992

Hans-Joachim Giersberg, Manfred Görtemaker, Frank Bauer, et al.: *Schloss Cecilienhof und die Potsdamer Konferenz 1945 – Von der Hohenzollernwohnung zur Gedenkstätte.* Berlin – Kleinmachnow – Potsdam, 1995

Michael Hassels: *Der Kronprinz privat. Zur Wiederherstellung neuer Museumsräume im Schloss Cecilienhof, Museumsjournal*, no. 2/10, Berlin, 1996

Heiner Timmermann (ed.): *Potsdam 1945: Konzept, Taktik, Irrtum?*, Berlin, 1997

Jörg Kirschstein: *Kronprinzessin Cecilie – Eine Bildbiographie*, Berlin, 2004

Heike Müller, Harald Berndt: *Schloss Cecilienhof und die Konferenz von Potsdam 1945*, Potsdam, 2006

Harald Berndt, Jörg Kirschstein: *Schloss Cecilienhof – Tudorromantik und Weltpolitik.* Munich, Berlin, London, New York, 2008

Matthias Uhl: *Die Teilung Deutschlands*. Berlin – Brandenburg, 2009

Photos: Bildarchiv SPSG / Fotografen: Wolfgang Pfauder, Daniel Lindner, Roland Handrick, Hans Bach, Hagen Immel, Dr. Peter Michael Bauers; Bildagentur Ullstein Bild Berlin (p. 2 at the bottom); Bildagentur Preußischer Kulturbesitz, Berlin (p. 4 at the bottom); Sammlung Jörg Kirschstein, Potsdam (p. 6, p. 9), Klaus Lehnart, Berlin (back cover); Bildarchiv Harry S. Truman Library and Museum, Independence, USA (p. 15, p. 19, p. 21, p. 24/25, p. 26, p. 29); Bildarchiv Imperial War Museum, London, UK (p. 13)
Maps: SPSG / Bearbeiter: Beate Laus; DKV / Bearbeiter: Birgit Gric (p. 11, p. 18)

Imprint

Published by the Stiftung Preußische Schlösser und Gärten Berlin-Brandenburg (SPSG)
Texts: Harald Berndt (palace), Matthias Simmich (Potsdam Conference)
Editing (German): Luzie Diekmann
English translations: Catherine Framm
Layout: Hendrik Bäßler, Berlin
Coordination: Elvira Kühn
Printing: DZA Druckerei zu Altenburg GmbH, Altenburg

The Deutsche Nationalbibliothek (German National Library) lists this publication in the Deutsche Nationalbibliografie; detailed bibliographic data are available on the Internet: http://dnb.d-nb.de.

ISBN 978-3-422-98253-6